**Editor**
Eric Migliaccio

**Illustrator**
Clint McKnight

**Cover Artist**
Brenda DiAntonis

**Editor in Chief**
Ina Massler Levin, M.A.

**Creative Director**
Karen J. Goldfluss, M.S. Ed.

**Art Coordinator**
Renée Christine Yates

**Imaging**
Rosa C. See

*Publisher*
*Mary D. Smith, M.S. Ed.*

TCR 2918

# Paired Passages
## Linking Fact to Fiction

CORRELATED TO COMMON CORE STANDARDS

- Learn to differentiate between nonfiction and fiction.
- Build reading comprehension and critical thinking.
- See how fiction and nonfiction can be connected.
- Synthesize information from two contrasting passages.

Teacher Created Resources

**Author**

Ruth Foster, M.Ed.

**Teacher Created Resources, Inc.**
6421 Industry Way
Westminster, CA 92683
www.teachercreated.com

ISBN: 978-1-4206-2918-7

©2009 Teacher Created Resources, Inc.
Reprinted, 2013
Made in U.S.A.

Teacher Created Resources

# Table of Contents

# Introduction

> *It was Buddy, an 18 month old German shepherd, who had contacted 911.*
>
> *\*\*\*\*\**
>
> *Pennsylvania was besieged by a rodent epidemic so large that they had to import cats!*

If a student read either one of these statements out of context, the student might have a difficult time knowing which statement is fiction and which one is nonfiction. In addition, the student would have no idea how the two statements could be tied together or used to support an argument or idea.

If, on the other hand, the student read these statements in context and understood how they fit into an entire passage, the student would be able to answer with confidence that, as strange as it may seem, a man who suffered from massive seizures had trained his assistance dog to press programmed telephone buttons until a 911 operator came on line and responded. The student would then be able to compare, contrast, or tie this fact to a fictitious passage where one character uses historical facts to prove that domesticated cats are overlooked American heroes. (Both passages deal with helpful domestic animals.)

The assessment sections of many state tests now contain paired passages. After reading two passages, students are expected to differentiate between fiction and nonfiction passages. They are expected to see how the two are connected and understand the underlying connection, as well as how they are dissimilar. They are expected to demonstrate their understanding of the passages by answering multiple-choice questions, as well as by providing written responses.

This is a multileveled task that draws on many different aspects of the reading and writing process. *Paired Passages: Linking Fact to Fiction* was written to provide practice with this type of exercise and assessment. It provides the following:

- ⁘ exercises that build reading comprehension
- ⁘ exercises that develop the skills needed to break down and analyze story elements
- ⁘ exercises that provide practice in keeping sequence and details from two sources separate
- ⁘ exercises that provide practice in proper letter formation, spacing, and spelling
- ⁘ practice with multiple-choice questions
- ⁘ practice with written-response questions on individual-passage themes
- ⁘ practice with written-response questions that utilize information from two contrasting passages.

# Introduction (cont.)

In short, *Paired Passages: Linking Fact to Fiction* was written so that students will develop and practice the skills it takes to compare and contrast fiction and nonfiction passages. If asked, "Is it true that a dog named Buddy contacted 911?" students will know how to find and use information from two given passages to answer the question. They will also be able to record their reasoned response in the written form.

## The Stories

There are 25 units in *Paired Passages: Linking Fact to Fiction.* Each individual unit contains two high-interest passages. The first passage is nonfiction, and the second is fiction. Each passage is written at grade level and contains appropriate vocabulary and sentence structure. The passages are tied together with a common theme. Unit subjects run the gamut from golf courses covered in red crabs to a man who jumped from the stratosphere. The units may be done sequentially, but they do not have to be. A teacher may choose to go out of order or pick specific units at different times because of class interest or individual students' needs. Units may be done as a class, or they may be assigned as individual work.

## The Multiple-Choice Questions

A page of multiple-choice questions follows the two passages. The first question focuses on the nonfiction passage, and the second question focuses on the fiction passage. Answer choices for both these questions come only from the passage to which the question stem is referring.

The third multiple-choice question asks what both passages have in common. The fourth and fifth questions require the student to differentiate between the passages and understand what topic is covered in each one, as the answer choices are drawn from both passages. A few of these questions will require students to combine the information from both passages to infer or extrapolate the answer.

Students can answer multiple-choice questions on the page by filling in the circle of the correct answer. Students can also answer multiple-choice questions by filling in the answer sheet located on page 7. Using this page provides practice responding in a standardized-test format.

## The Written Responses

A page requiring written responses makes up the final page of each unit. The first two exercises vary, depending on the unit. They may require sequencing of events by filling in boxes, making lists, or drawing and labeling a picture. Each response deals with only one of the passages. These exercises are written to provide students with a foundation of sorting and organizing information. They provide an exercise in referring back to and keeping two different pieces of literary prose separate in the reader's mind.

The final two written responses require higher-level responses. First, one is asked to write out the main theme of each passage with three complete sentences. Lastly, one is asked to write a paragraph in response to a question that requires thinking about or using information from both passages to answer.

A teacher's expectations of what is a satisfactory response on these last questions may change over the year, or it may vary depending on the level of the student. For example, at the beginning of the year or with some students, a teacher may accept phonetic spelling and the lack of some kinds of punctuation. As specific topics are covered in class and students mature, a teacher may begin to check spelling, punctuation, grammar, and sentence construction more rigorously and require longer and more detailed responses. Enough variation allows that all students, even those deficient in grade-level writing skills or those with advanced writing skills, can participate.

# Meeting Standards

Each passage and question in *Paired Passages: Linking Fact to Fiction* meets one or more of the following Common Core State Standards © Copyright 2010. National Governors Association Center for Best Practices and Council of Chief State School Officers. All rights reserved. For more information about the Common Core State Standards, go to *http://www.corestandards.org/*.

| Literature Standards | Passage Title | Pages |
|---|---|---|
| **Key Ideas and Details** | | |
| **Standard 1**: RL.8.1. Cite the textual evidence that most strongly supports an analysis of what the text says explicitly as well as inferences drawn from the text. | all passages | |
| **Standard 2**: RL.8.2. Determine a theme or central idea of a text and analyze its development over the course of the text, including its relationship to the characters, setting, and plot; provide an objective summary of the text. | all passages | |
| **Standard 3**: RL.8.3. Analyze how particular lines of dialogue or incidents in a story or drama propel the action, reveal aspects of a character, or provoke a decision. | What It Takes to Win<br>French Fire Words<br>An End to the Story<br>Scorpion Charlatan<br>Jungle Friend<br>Jolon's Hero<br>All Things Vanilla<br>Why the Doctor Didn't Vote<br>How It Went<br>Letter from an Exchange Student<br>Marathon Training Journal<br>Scoop of the Century!<br>Hamaguchi's Sacrifice | 13–15<br>29–31<br>49–51<br>53–55<br>65–67<br>73–75<br>77–79<br>85–87<br>89–91<br>93–95<br>97–99<br>101–103<br>105–107 |
| **Craft and Structure** | | |
| **Standard 4**: RL.8.4. Determine the meaning of words and phrases as they are used in a text, including figurative and connotative meanings; analyze the impact of specific word choices on meaning and tone, including analogies or allusions to other texts. | all passages | |
| **Standard 5**: RL.8.5. Compare and contrast the structure of two or more texts and analyze how the differing structure of each text contributes to its meaning and style. | What Madeline Found Good<br>Body Math<br>Scorpion Charlatan<br>Jungle Friend<br>Jolon's Hero<br>Why the Doctor Didn't Vote<br>How It Went<br>Letter from an Exchange Student<br>Marathon Training Journal<br>Scoop of the Century!<br>Hamaguchi's Sacrifice | 41–43<br>45–47<br>53–55<br>65–67<br>73–75<br>85–87<br>89–91<br>93–95<br>97–99<br>101–103<br>105–107 |
| **Standard 6**: RL.8.6. Analyze how differences in the points of view of the characters and the audience or reader (e.g., created through the use of dramatic irony) create such effects as suspense or humor. | When Sandals Are Not Fine<br>An Even Trade for Style<br>Scoop of the Century!<br>Hamaguchi's Sacrifice | 9–11<br>57–59<br>101–103<br>105–107 |

# Meeting Standards *(cont.)*

| Integration of Knowledge and Ideas | | |
|---|---|---|
| **Standard 9**: RL.8.9. Analyze how a modern work of fiction draws on themes, patterns of events, or character types from myths, traditional stories, or religious works such as the Bible, including describing how the material is rendered new. | A Folktale from Thailand | 33–35 |

| Range of Reading and Level of Text Complexity | | |
|---|---|---|
| **Standard 10**: RL.8.10. By the end of the year, read and comprehend literature, including stories, dramas, and poems, at the high end of grades 6–8 text complexity band independently and proficiently. | all passages | |

| **Informational Text Standards** | **Passage Title** | **Pages** |
|---|---|---|
| Key Ideas and Details | | |
| **Standard 1**: RI.8.1. Cite the textual evidence that most strongly supports an analysis of what the text says explicitly as well as inferences drawn from the text. | all passages | |
| **Standard 2**: RI.8.2. Determine a central idea of a text and analyze its development over the course of the text, including its relationship to supporting ideas; provide an objective summary of the text. | all passages | |
| **Standard 3**: RI.8.3. Analyze how a text makes connections among and distinctions between individuals, ideas, or events (e.g., through comparisons, analogies, or categories). | A Tribe for the Gullible<br>When a Hair Is Big<br>A Lifesaving Fire<br>Scorpion Scientist<br>State Quarters<br>Jumping from the Stratosphere<br>A Conundrum on the Nazca Plain<br>A Lifetime of Names<br>Masters of Understatement<br>Flying Blood<br>Tsunami Survivor | 16–19<br>24–27<br>28–31<br>52–55<br>68–71<br>72–75<br>80–83<br>84–87<br>88–91<br>100–103<br>104–107 |
| Craft and Structure | | |
| **Standard 4**: RI.8.4. Determine the meaning of words and phrases as they are used in a text, including figurative, connotative, and technical meanings; analyze the impact of specific word choices on meaning and tone, including analogies or allusions to other texts. | all passages | |
| **Standard 5**: RI.8.5. Analyze in detail the structure of a specific paragraph in a text, including the role of particular sentences in developing and refining a key concept. | Why the Doctor Shocked<br>Missing for 28 Years<br>State Quarters<br>Jumping from the Stratosphere<br>A Lifetime of Names<br>Masters of Understatement<br>Flying Blood | 56–59<br>64–67<br>68–71<br>72–75<br>84–87<br>88–91<br>100–103 |
| Range of Reading and Level of Text Complexity | | |
| **Standard 10**: RI.8.10. By the end of the year, read and comprehend literary nonfiction at the high end of the grades 6–8 text complexity band independently and proficiently. | all passages | |

# Answer Sheets

**page** _____

1. Ⓐ Ⓑ Ⓒ Ⓓ
2. Ⓐ Ⓑ Ⓒ Ⓓ
3. Ⓐ Ⓑ Ⓒ Ⓓ
4. Ⓐ Ⓑ Ⓒ Ⓓ
5. Ⓐ Ⓑ Ⓒ Ⓓ

**page** _____

1. Ⓐ Ⓑ Ⓒ Ⓓ
2. Ⓐ Ⓑ Ⓒ Ⓓ
3. Ⓐ Ⓑ Ⓒ Ⓓ
4. Ⓐ Ⓑ Ⓒ Ⓓ
5. Ⓐ Ⓑ Ⓒ Ⓓ

**page** _____

1. Ⓐ Ⓑ Ⓒ Ⓓ
2. Ⓐ Ⓑ Ⓒ Ⓓ
3. Ⓐ Ⓑ Ⓒ Ⓓ
4. Ⓐ Ⓑ Ⓒ Ⓓ
5. Ⓐ Ⓑ Ⓒ Ⓓ

**page** _____

1. Ⓐ Ⓑ Ⓒ Ⓓ
2. Ⓐ Ⓑ Ⓒ Ⓓ
3. Ⓐ Ⓑ Ⓒ Ⓓ
4. Ⓐ Ⓑ Ⓒ Ⓓ
5. Ⓐ Ⓑ Ⓒ Ⓓ

**page** _____

1. Ⓐ Ⓑ Ⓒ Ⓓ
2. Ⓐ Ⓑ Ⓒ Ⓓ
3. Ⓐ Ⓑ Ⓒ Ⓓ
4. Ⓐ Ⓑ Ⓒ Ⓓ
5. Ⓐ Ⓑ Ⓒ Ⓓ

**page** _____

1. Ⓐ Ⓑ Ⓒ Ⓓ
2. Ⓐ Ⓑ Ⓒ Ⓓ
3. Ⓐ Ⓑ Ⓒ Ⓓ
4. Ⓐ Ⓑ Ⓒ Ⓓ
5. Ⓐ Ⓑ Ⓒ Ⓓ

**page** _____

1. Ⓐ Ⓑ Ⓒ Ⓓ
2. Ⓐ Ⓑ Ⓒ Ⓓ
3. Ⓐ Ⓑ Ⓒ Ⓓ
4. Ⓐ Ⓑ Ⓒ Ⓓ
5. Ⓐ Ⓑ Ⓒ Ⓓ

**page** _____

1. Ⓐ Ⓑ Ⓒ Ⓓ
2. Ⓐ Ⓑ Ⓒ Ⓓ
3. Ⓐ Ⓑ Ⓒ Ⓓ
4. Ⓐ Ⓑ Ⓒ Ⓓ
5. Ⓐ Ⓑ Ⓒ Ⓓ

**page** _____

1. Ⓐ Ⓑ Ⓒ Ⓓ
2. Ⓐ Ⓑ Ⓒ Ⓓ
3. Ⓐ Ⓑ Ⓒ Ⓓ
4. Ⓐ Ⓑ Ⓒ Ⓓ
5. Ⓐ Ⓑ Ⓒ Ⓓ

**page** _____

1. Ⓐ Ⓑ Ⓒ Ⓓ
2. Ⓐ Ⓑ Ⓒ Ⓓ
3. Ⓐ Ⓑ Ⓒ Ⓓ
4. Ⓐ Ⓑ Ⓒ Ⓓ
5. Ⓐ Ⓑ Ⓒ Ⓓ

**page** _____

1. Ⓐ Ⓑ Ⓒ Ⓓ
2. Ⓐ Ⓑ Ⓒ Ⓓ
3. Ⓐ Ⓑ Ⓒ Ⓓ
4. Ⓐ Ⓑ Ⓒ Ⓓ
5. Ⓐ Ⓑ Ⓒ Ⓓ

**page** _____

1. Ⓐ Ⓑ Ⓒ Ⓓ
2. Ⓐ Ⓑ Ⓒ Ⓓ
3. Ⓐ Ⓑ Ⓒ Ⓓ
4. Ⓐ Ⓑ Ⓒ Ⓓ
5. Ⓐ Ⓑ Ⓒ Ⓓ

**page** _____

1. Ⓐ Ⓑ Ⓒ Ⓓ
2. Ⓐ Ⓑ Ⓒ Ⓓ
3. Ⓐ Ⓑ Ⓒ Ⓓ
4. Ⓐ Ⓑ Ⓒ Ⓓ
5. Ⓐ Ⓑ Ⓒ Ⓓ

**page** _____

1. Ⓐ Ⓑ Ⓒ Ⓓ
2. Ⓐ Ⓑ Ⓒ Ⓓ
3. Ⓐ Ⓑ Ⓒ Ⓓ
4. Ⓐ Ⓑ Ⓒ Ⓓ
5. Ⓐ Ⓑ Ⓒ Ⓓ

**page** _____

1. Ⓐ Ⓑ Ⓒ Ⓓ
2. Ⓐ Ⓑ Ⓒ Ⓓ
3. Ⓐ Ⓑ Ⓒ Ⓓ
4. Ⓐ Ⓑ Ⓒ Ⓓ
5. Ⓐ Ⓑ Ⓒ Ⓓ

# Crab Hazards

When a golfer plays any golf course, he or she expects the course to be peppered with hazards like sand traps, woods, and ponds of water. There is one particular golf course, though, where along with these stationary hazards, the player must expect to contend with hundreds of moving hazards. The golf course is located on Christmas Island. Christmas Island is an external territory of Australia located in the Indian Ocean. The moving hazards are bright red, four-and-one-half-inch (11.4 cm) crabs.

Over 150 million of these brightly colored crabs inhabit the island's rainforests. Every year, starting around November, the crustaceans migrate. They exit the rainforest and make their way to the ocean to mate. The males return to the rainforest after mating. The females return about two weeks later after spawning up to 100,000 eggs.

The golf course on Christmas Island is located in the crabs' migration route. During migration season, the course is peppered with hundreds of the moving crustaceans. The rules of the Christmas Island Golf Club state that all players must treat the crabs as they would any other hazard. They cannot move them, and they must play around them. If a roving crustacean happens to knock a ball while it is on the green, tipping it into a hole, the ball is considered "in."

Just as the golfers must contend with a moving hazard, so must the crabs. As the island has developed, roads have been constructed that run through the crabs' migration route. Unfortunately, up to two million crabs are killed by passing vehicles every year. Residents of Christmas Island are trying to reduce the number by putting up "Crab Crossing" signs and closing certain roads during migration season.

# When Sandals Are Not Fine

Sebastian stepped off the tiny charter plane that had brought him to Christmas Island and felt the warm air waft over his skin. "My first trip south of the equator!" he thought to himself excitedly. "The seasons are opposite, so instead of November being a late-fall month like it is north of the equator, it's a late-spring month! I can practice my golf swing while people back home are raking leaves and beginning to bring out their winter jackets!"

That very afternoon, after quickly unpacking his duffel bag, Sebastian told his friend Indra that they should head to the golf course. "I don't mean to sound arrogant," Sebastian warned Indra, "but I'm an experienced golfer used to playing around difficult hazards. There's nothing here that I haven't seen before, so you shouldn't harbor any high expectations about beating me."

Indra laughed and said, "Sebastian, you're as competitive and arrogant as you've always been! Yes, let's play golf. But you should really change out of your sandals, because they're not appropriate."

Sebastian snorted and replied, "Indra, we're on a tiny speck of land in the middle of the Indian Ocean. It's not like we're playing in a high-scale world competition where we have to adhere to a dress code. I'm not changing for this easy, low-class course."

Indra said, "Sebastian, listen to me, you really need to change into covered shoes because—"

"Don't be ridiculous," Sebastian said, cutting Indra off in mid-sentence. "I'm on vacation, and sandals are fine, so promise me you won't say another word until after the game."

Shrugging, Indra nodded in agreement. Once at the golf course, Indra kept his promise and didn't utter a word, even as Sebastian yelped and danced in fear as bright red crustaceans crawled toward his uncovered and unprotected toes.

# Show What You Know

*The following are questions based on the passages "Crab Hazards" and "When Sandals Are Not Fine." If needed, you may look back at the passages to answer the questions.*

1. **If a golfer on Christmas Island does not hit a ball in a hole but the ball is "in," it is most likely**

   Ⓐ June.

   Ⓑ August.

   Ⓒ September.

   Ⓓ November.

2. **Indra did not make a sound as the crustaceans crawled toward Sebastian because he**

   Ⓐ was not arrogant.

   Ⓑ had told Sebastian not to wear sandals.

   Ⓒ had promised Sebastian he would not say a word.

   Ⓓ knew that Sebastian was used to all types of hazards.

3. **What did you read about in both stories?**

   Ⓐ protecting crabs

   Ⓑ golf dress codes

   Ⓒ crab expectations

   Ⓓ golf-course hazards

4. **From the stories, one can tell that most likely members of the Christmas Island Golf Club were**

   Ⓐ better golf players than Sebastian.

   Ⓑ more practiced golf players than Sebastian.

   Ⓒ more familiar with some hazards than Sebastian.

   Ⓓ not as willing to adhere to a dress code as Sebastian.

5. **Sebastian might have been more comfortable wearing sandals at the golf course if**

   Ⓐ he had visited Christmas Island in January.

   Ⓑ the dress code had been different.

   Ⓒ Indra had told him about the crabs.

   Ⓓ he had seen the "Crab Crossing" signs.

# Show What You Know (cont.)

6. **Contrast the moving hazards on Christmas Island.**

| | For People | For Crabs |
|---|---|---|
| Hazard | | |
| How dealt with | | |

7. **Fill in the chart with the names of the correct seasons.**

| Begin Date | March 21 | June 21 | Sept. 21 | Dec. 21 |
|---|---|---|---|---|
| North of the equator | | | | |
| South of the equator | | | | |

**Write three or four sentences that tell what each story is about.**

8. **"Crab Hazards"**

_____

_____

_____

9. **"When Sandals Are Not Fine"**

_____

_____

_____

10. **Imagine you are competing in a match at the Christmas Island Golf Club. You lose only because the person you are playing against has a ball knocked into a hole by a crab. Describe how you might feel about the fairness of the match. Include some facts about Christmas Island and the crustaceans found on it in your answer.** *(Use a separate piece of paper. Your writing should be a few paragraphs long.)*

# The Most Daring Move

What was called "the most daring move ever seen on track" occurred on August 4, 1936, in Berlin, Germany. The "move" was performed by John Woodruff, a black American competitor, in the middle of the 800-meter running race at the 1936 Olympic Games. Young and inexperienced, Woodruff was only a 21-year-old college freshman when he earned his spot on the United States Olympic team.

At the start of the race, the 6-foot 3-inch (2 m) tall Woodruff became trapped, boxed in by the more experienced runners. All the spectators assumed Woodruff would lose. He was surrounded, and if he broke between the two leaders, he would be disqualified with a foul. Woodruff may have been an inexperienced novice, but he was a quick thinker. He made a decision, and as the crowd gasped in disbelief, he acted on it.

Woodruff came to a complete stop. After waiting until all the other runners in the pack had passed him, he quickly moved to an outside lane. Once alone and in the outer lane, Woodruff charged for the winner's tape that stretched across the finish line. As the roars of the astonished crowd filled the stadium, Woodruff extended his stride so that it measured nearly 10 feet (3 m), and with a burst of speed he took the lead. Woodruff was victorious, with a winning time of 1 minute, 52.9 seconds.

Woodruff's gold medal win went down in history because of his daring move, but it was also significant for another reason. At that time, Adolf Hitler, Germany's leader, was pushing his "master race" agenda. Though U.S. leaders considered boycotting the games to show that they thought this was wrong, the United States was racially segregated. Woodruff's gold medal, as well as the gold medals won by his fellow black teammate Jesse Owens, showed those with prejudice that ability and superiority have nothing to do with skin color.

# What It Takes to Win

The roar of the spectators filled the stadium, but Benjamin was oblivious to the sound. He heard nothing but the pounding of his own heart. An experienced and professional runner, Benjamin had been training for years. Now, at the age of 25, Benjamin was sure that his dedication would pay off and all of his training would lead him to victory. Yes, in just a few minutes, as soon as the starting gun was fired, Benjamin would finish the 800-meter run in record time and stand on the winner's podium to accept his Olympic gold medal.

When the starting gun was fired, Benjamin's body sprang to action with the suddeness of a well-oiled steel spring. He ran with the speed and muscled grace of a cheetah closing in on its prey. Confident of his form, he moved to the inner lane and picked up his speed. At the half-lap mark, Benjamin lengthened his stride and prepared to take the lead. Yes, as his powerful legs and arms moved in a fluid motion, Benjamin remained confident that he had the strength, endurance, and speed to win.

No, Benjamin did not move to the front of the pack. Instead, he began to panic as he realized that he was trapped. Somehow, Benjamin had gotten boxed in. Breaking between the two runners in front of him would get Benjamin disqualified on a foul, and there was no way around the runners next to him who were waiting for an opportunity to edge up on the pack and overtake the lead, too.

Understanding too well the seriousness of his predicament, Benjamin concluded that he had lost the gold. A professional to the core, Benjamin concentrated on what was obtainable: a third place finish and a bronze medal.

# Show What You Know

*The following are questions based on the passages "The Most Daring Move" and "What It Takes to Win." If needed, you may look back at the passages to answer the questions.*

1. **One could say that when Woodruff made his move, it was like giving the other runners**

   Ⓐ a foul.
   Ⓑ an affront.
   Ⓒ a head start.
   Ⓓ a spot in an outer lane.

2. **Benjamin concluded that he had lost the gold because he did not think**

   Ⓐ he had trained enough.
   Ⓑ he could lengthen his stride.
   Ⓒ he was as fast as the two leaders.
   Ⓓ he could escape from being boxed in.

3. **What do both stories have in common?**

   Ⓐ daring runners
   Ⓑ Olympic runners
   Ⓒ disqualified runners
   Ⓓ inexperienced runners

4. **From the stories, one can tell that**

   Ⓐ runners can be disqualified.
   Ⓑ only daring runners win gold medals.
   Ⓒ runners always want the inside lane.
   Ⓓ older runners have an edge over younger runners.

5. **The word "novice" from the story "The Most Daring Move" is the opposite of what word from the story "What It Takes to Win?"**

   Ⓐ winner
   Ⓑ oblivious
   Ⓒ spectator
   Ⓓ experienced

14

# Show What You Know *(cont.)*

6. **Tell what the numbers mentioned in the story "The Most Daring Move" refer to.**

| | |
|---|---|
| 4 | |
| 1936 | |
| 21 | |
| 6 3 | |
| 10 | |
| 1:52.9 | |

7. **For each paragraph in the story "What It Takes to Win" write down if you think the author expected you to believe Benjamin would win a gold medal. Write down a phrase or part of a sentence from the paragraph that supports your answer.**

| *Paragraph 1* | *Paragraph 2* | *Paragraph 3* | *Paragraph 4* |
|---|---|---|---|
| | | | |

**Write three or four sentences that tell what each story is about.**

8. **"The Most Daring Move"**

_____

_____

_____

9. **"What It Takes to Win"**

_____

_____

_____

10. **Think about a time when you did something unexpected and daring. (Your daring move could be about sports, food, dress, society, or anything else you can think of.) Describe what you did, how people reacted, and what happened because of your daring move.** *(Use a separate piece of paper. Your writing should be a few paragraphs long.)*

# A Tribe for the Gullible

In 1971, anthropologists announced an amazing find. An isolated and primitive tribe had just been discovered. The tribe was located deep in the jungles of the Philippines. Anthropologists study mankind, especially its origin, development, divisions, and customs. The Tasadays presented an amazing opportunity to study a tribe that was, as one anthropologist said with excitement, "still in the Stone Age."

There were 26 Tasadays. They dressed in simple loincloths and skirts of orchid leaves. Their only tools were scrapers, stone axes, digging sticks, and drills for making fire. They lived in caves and worked together as a group. They spent many hours of each day singing, telling stories, or sleeping. Books were printed about the Tasadays. Photographs appeared in *National Geographic*'s August 1972 issue. A major television studio gave $50,000 for a documentary to be made.

Despite the world's interest in the Tasadays, some anthropologists began to get suspicious. They wondered how it was possible for the Tasadays to have stayed isolated for so long. They wondered why the Tasadays were not like other primitive people. They wondered if people interested in the Tasadays were being too gullible. They wondered if people were too easily being tricked and that the Tasadays were nothing but a big hoax.

The government of the Philippines stopped allowing anthropologists to study the Tasadays. All contact stopped for over 14 years. When the government changed, a Swiss journalist went in search of the Tasadays. The journalist discovered that people had indeed been gullible. The Stone Age Tasadays were not real. They had only pretended to be a lost, primitive tribe. In real life, they wore clothes and slept on beds. The person who "discovered" them initially had hoped to make large profits off of his scam.

# Sale for the Gullible

Cassandra was an art appraiser known for her honesty and depth of knowledge. Museum curators trusted her. If Cassandra said a picture was worth a million dollars, it sold for a million dollars.

One day Cassandra got a call from the curator of a very famous and prestigious museum. The curator said, "I'd like to procure a particular painting for the museum from the late 14th century. The seller says he stumbled upon it hidden in a cellar deep in the Italian countryside. If it's authentic, it's truly a remarkable find."

"You have doubts?" queried Cassandra.

"I can't explain why, but yes," replied the museum curator. "I have tests proving that the paint and canvas correlate with the 14th century, but you and I know that determined and knowledgeable counterfeiters can concoct their own paints, as well as reuse authentic canvases."

"What does it look like?" Cassandra asked.

"Oh," said the curator, his voice brightening, "it's a marvelously detailed scene of a village getting ready for a wedding party. The bride is draped in lacy finery, peasants are dancing boisterously, and in the background one can see several women watching the merriment as they take bright red tomatoes from a basket and mash them into a sauce. All the costumes, furniture, and even the art techniques that went into the painting match the time period and the region where it was found."

"It's a sale only for the gullible buyer," Cassandra interrupted.

"What?" asked the curator, his voice surprised and shocked. "How can you know? You haven't even seen the painting!"

"What I do know," answered Cassandra, "is that the tomato is a New World plant that originated in South America. Most likely, it was first taken to Europe from Mexico during the first half of the 16th century."

# Show What You Know

*The following are questions based on the passages "A Tribe for the Gullible" and "Sale for the Gullible." If needed, you may look back at the passages to answer the questions.*

1. **Anthropologists were interested in studying the Tasadays because they wanted**

   (A) to make a documentary.

   (B) to study jungle orchid plants.

   (C) to know why they were so gullible.

   (D) to learn about their stories and beliefs.

2. **Cassandra would not have been able to tell that the painting wasn't authentic if**

   (A) she had seen it.

   (B) it had been sold in Mexico.

   (C) Italy was part of the New World.

   (D) tomatoes were brought to Europe in the 17th century.

3. **What do both stories have in common?**

   (A) a hoax

   (B) a curator

   (C) an appraiser

   (D) an anthropologist

4. **Which statement is not true?**

   (A) There were 26 Tasadays.

   (B) The Tasadays had stone axes.

   (C) The Tasadays wore loincloths.

   (D) The Tasadays were an authentic tribe.

5. **A gullible person might believe he or she**

   (A) can view the Brooklyn Bridge.

   (B) can procure the Brooklyn Bridge.

   (C) can drive on the Brooklyn Bridge.

   (D) can photograph the Brooklyn Bridge.

# Show What You Know *(cont.)*

6. **Write down the three ways mentioned in the story that people who weren't anthropologists might have first learned about the Tasadays.**

   _____

   _____

   _____

   • Would you believe a story if it was in all three of these sources?     *no*     *yes*

   • What might make you doubt it?

   _____

7. **Fill in the blanks with information from the story "Sale for the Gullible."**

   **a.** Why did people trust Cassandra?

   _____

   **b.** Who called Cassandra?

   _____

   **c.** Where was the picture found?

   _____

   **d.** What was in the painting's background?

   _____

   **e.** How did Cassandra know it wasn't authentic?

   _____

   **f.** When were tomatoes brought to Europe?

   _____

**Write three or four sentences that tell what each story is about.**

8. **"A Tribe for the Gullible"**

   _____

   _____

   _____

9. **"Sale for the Gullible"**

   _____

   _____

   _____

10. **Think of a time when you were gullible or a time when someone you know or read about was gullible. Describe the situation, prank, or hoax, and what happened.**
    *(Use a separate piece of paper. Your writing should be a few paragraphs long.)*

# Carpet Tacks and a Goat

On April 24, 1895, Joshua Slocum embarked on a voyage. Sailing on a 36' 9" (11.2 m) ship that he had rebuilt, he set off to be the first person to circumnavigate the globe alone. Slocum was successful on his solo venture, completing the trip on June 27, 1898.

Slocum wrote a book about his 46,000-mile (73,600 km) trip around the world. The book is filled with Slocum's adventures and thoughts, but it also talks about two gifts Slocum received. The first gift was a box of carpet tacks that ended up saving Slocum's life.

Slocum was attempting to cross the Strait of Magellan. The Strait of Magellan is a narrow, treacherous stretch of water at the southern tip of South America. Danger came from fierce winds, as well as native bandits who made a practice of robbing ships. Desperate for sleep one night, Slocum anchored near shore. He was awakened by howls of pain and the splash of people jumping directly into the sea. The carpet tacks Slocum had strewn all over the deck had deterred the would-be thieves!

The second gift was a goat, given to him on a tiny speck of land in the middle of the vast southern Atlantic Ocean. Slocum was told that the goat would be as companionable as a dog. Previously, Slocum had thought about bringing a dog for company, but he had decided against it because of space limitations and fear of rabies. (Vaccinations against rabies and a cure for it did not yet exist.) After the goat feasted on Slocum's charts, sea jacket, and hat, Slocum wrote that the goat was no better than a pirate, and it was with great relief that he left it at the next island he stopped at.

# A Fictitious Blog

**Blog of Kenneth Hobart**

*February 5, 2009*

As I weigh anchor tonight in the Strait of Magellan, I can't help but think how different it was for Slocum. Although I'm following his footsteps, circumnavigating the globe solo, I have a motor, satellite radio, computer, generator, and GPS tracking system on my ship. Slocum's Spray was equipped with nothing but sails.

I've found the people of Tierra del Fuego to be kind and hospitable. Slocum's experience with the native Fuegians was quite different. In the book he wrote to describe his adventures (there were no blogs in Slocum's time!), Slocum tells how he thwarted an attack.

It was daylight, and Slocum spotted from afar canoes filled with hostile Fuegians heading toward the Spray. One would think that Slocum would have no chance of escape, it being one against many; but thanks to Slocum's preparing ahead, the Fuegians retreated after never getting closer than 300 feet (91 m).

The Fuegians retreated because they believed Slocum's boat to be crewed by a band of cutthroats! Slocum had stuck seafaring scarecrows he had made and dressed in his own clothes out of every hatch and porthole, and as he fired shots across the bows of the oncoming canoes, he made the scarecrows move by pulling on strings he had attached to them.

In his book, Slocum described being caught at one point, but it wasn't by inhospitable people. While in this treacherous strait, he made six attempts to sail out of the very cove I'm currently anchored in. Six times fierce winds blew him back, and one time he was blown so close to shore that his boat became caught in a tree!

Slocum's book set me off on an adventure. May this blog do the same for someone else.

# Show What You Know

*The following are questions based on the passages "Carpet Tacks and a Goat" and "A Fictitious Blog." If needed, you may look back at the passages to answer the questions.*

1. **About how long did it take for Slocum to circumnavigate the globe?**

   Ⓐ  3 years 2 months 2 days

   Ⓑ  3 years 2 months 3 days

   Ⓒ  4 years 2 months 2 days

   Ⓓ  4 years 2 months 3 days

2. **Think about how the word *hospitable* relates to *inhospitable*. Which two words relate in the same way?**

   *hospitable : inhospitable*

   Ⓐ  friendly : hostile

   Ⓑ  native : seafaring

   Ⓒ  treacherous : welcoming

   Ⓓ  seafaring : circumnavigating

3. **What do both stories have in common?**

   Ⓐ  sailors who met with hostile natives

   Ⓑ  sailors who traveled with companions

   Ⓒ  sailors who circumnavigated the globe

   Ⓓ  sailors who followed in each other's footsteps

4. **From the stories, one can tell that**

   Ⓐ  goats are not native to Tierra Del Fuego.

   Ⓑ  Tierra Del Fuego is a treacherous country.

   Ⓒ  all natives of Tierra Del Fuego are hostile.

   Ⓓ  Tierra Del Fuego borders the Strait of Magellan.

5. **What might make Hobart, the fictitious blog writer, more willing than Slocum to have a dog with him?**

   Ⓐ  Dogs do not eat clothing.

   Ⓑ  A dog would take up less space now.

   Ⓒ  Dogs can be vaccinated against rabies now.

   Ⓓ  A dog would thwart a band of attacking cutthroats.

# Show What You Know (cont.)

6. Decide which of the gifts described in the story "Carpet Tacks and a Goat" was the best and worst. Briefly jot down why.

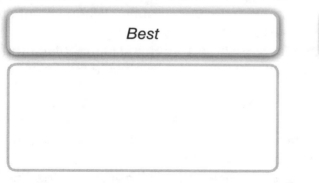

| Best | Worst |
|------|-------|
|      |       |

7. List the steps Slocum took to thwart an attack.

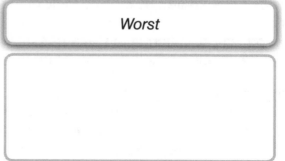

1.

2. attached strings to the scarecrows

4.

3.

Write three or four sentences that tell what each story is about.

8. "Carpet Tacks and a Goat"

_____

_____

_____

9. "A Fictitious Blog"

_____

_____

_____

10. Slocum could not write a blog, but he may have kept a journal. Write a possible journal entry for Slocum. You may use information from either story in your journal entry, or you may make up a completely new adventure. *(Use a separate piece of paper. Your journal entry should be a few paragraphs long.)*

# When a Hair Is Big

Nanotechnology is a new scientific field. It is a field that deals with the ultra-small. New things are created by moving individual atoms and molecules around. When something is manufactured with nanotechnology, it is not made from already existing materials such as wood, stone, cotton, metal, leather, or even plastic. When something is manufactured using nanotechnology, the new item or material is built atom by atom, molecule by molecule.

In nanotechnology, scientists use the nanoscale. The unit of measurement in the nanoscale is a nanometer. A nanometer (nm) is 1 billionth of a meter. To get an idea of how small a nanometer is, look at one of your hairs. Most likely, your strand of hair doesn't seem that thick. On the nanoscale, a hair is quite big. How large is it? It is 40,000 nanometers thick! Even a red blood cell is quite big on the nanoscale. How large is it? It measures 7,500 nanometers across!

Until recently, it was thought impossible that people could control how atoms and molecules are put together. The idea of making an object from the ground up was only a topic for science fiction. One reason the field became possible was the development of new microscopes. The microscopes were very powerful, and they were equipped with finely tipped probes. The microscopes made it possible for scientists to move around atoms and deal with structures, devices, and systems 1 to 100 nanometers in size.

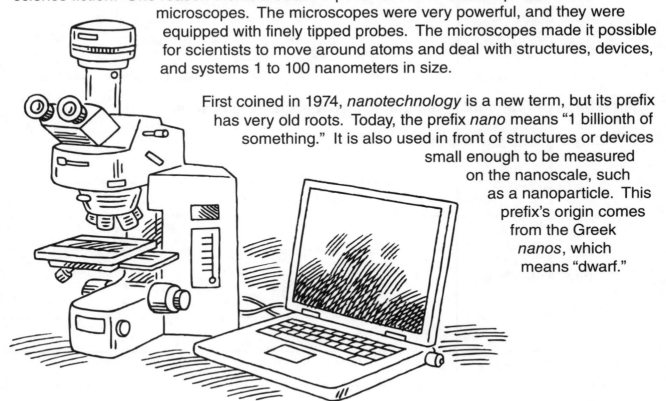

First coined in 1974, *nanotechnology* is a new term, but its prefix has very old roots. Today, the prefix *nano* means "1 billionth of something." It is also used in front of structures or devices small enough to be measured on the nanoscale, such as a nanoparticle. This prefix's origin comes from the Greek *nanos*, which means "dwarf."

# Out of the Dark Ages

Dr. Leonardo looked up from the chart of the patient sitting nervously in front of her. "The results of the body scans are in," she said, "and you have a cranial blood clot that is affecting the blood supply to your brain."

The patient, already pale, grew noticeably more ashen. "Doctor," he said, his voice trembling, "this doesn't sound good."

Picking up a syringe, Dr. Leonardo walked over to her patient and said, "You'll begin to suffer extreme and irreversible brain damage if the cranial clot isn't dissolved immediately. That's why it's imperative that we begin treatment now. This is going to sting a bit, but just lie back and try and relax."

"What's the injection for?" asked the patient. "Is it to put me to sleep so you can operate?"

"Operate?" laughed Dr. Leonardo as she carefully injected the contents of the syringe into the patient's right arm. "The time for that is past. I'm injecting a nanoscale robot, or

nanobot, into your vein. The nanobot is an advanced nanomachine that will travel through your bloodstream, hitching a ride on a red blood cell and directing it to the blood clot in your cranium. Once the nanobot hits the obstruction, it will dissolve the clot and continue its ride through the circulatory system while it breaks down and is absorbed by the body."

"But what if before it is absorbed the nanobot mistakenly thinks a vital part of my body is an obstruction and dissolves it?" asked the patient nervously.

"Don't worry," laughed Dr. Leonardo. "The nanobot has been precisely manufactured, atom by atom. It can only react to a cranial blood clot. What time do you think this is, the Dark Ages, when primitive surgeons put people to sleep and used sharp scalpels to make incisions like in the year 2010?"

# Show What You Know

*The following are questions based on the passages "When a Hair Is Big" and "Out of the Dark Ages." If needed, you may look back at the passages to answer the questions.*

1. **A nanosecond is**

   Ⓐ 1 billion seconds.

   Ⓑ 100 billion seconds.

   Ⓒ 1 billionth of a second.

   Ⓓ 100 billionths of a second.

2. **When something is imperative,**

   Ⓐ it must be done.

   Ⓑ it is irreversible.

   Ⓒ it can be dissolved.

   Ⓓ it is part of the cranium.

3. **What do both stories have in common?**

   Ⓐ They both explain the nanoscale.

   Ⓑ They both deal with nanotechnology.

   Ⓒ They both explain what nanobots are.

   Ⓓ They both deal with manufacturing atoms.

4. **From the stories, one can tell that the powerful microscopes that helped the field of nanotechnology develop may one day**

   Ⓐ be equipped with nanobots.

   Ⓑ be thought of as primitive.

   Ⓒ be used to dissolve blood clots.

   Ⓓ be manufactured with nanotechnology.

5. **"Out of the Dark Ages" could be considered a science fiction story because it deals with**

   Ⓐ the ultra-small.

   Ⓑ a new scientific field.

   Ⓒ a device not yet possible.

   Ⓓ dissolving something atom by atom.

# Show What You Know *(cont.)*

6. List three bits of information about the prefix *nano*.

   a. _____

   b. _____

   c. _____

7. Mark on the patient the possible locations of the blood clot and injection site.

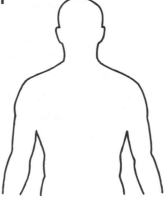

Write three or four sentences that tell what each story is about.

8. "When a Hair Is Big"

   _____

   _____

   _____

9. "Out of the Dark Ages"

   _____

   _____

   _____

10. Think of something that we use today that was once considered to be impossible or science fiction. Describe the device and how it has changed how we do things. Possible writing topics are telephones, cars, airplanes, rockets, refrigerators, air conditioners, computers, e-mail, television, microwave ovens, x-rays, etc. *(Use a separate piece of paper. Your writing should be a few paragraphs long.)*

# A Lifesaving Fire

Fifteen firefighters, specialized smokejumpers, parachuted into Mann Gulch on August 5, 1949. When the Montana firefighters started down the gulch, a breeze was blowing the fire away from them. Suddenly, as the wind reversed, the fire leaped across the gulch. An updraft and fierce winds caused the fire to shoot up. The firefighters were in grave danger. They were facing a wall of flame 50 feet (15 m) tall and 300 feet (91 m) deep that was hurtling toward them at a speed of 700 feet (213 m) per minute.

The firefighters dropped their gear and ran for their lives. When the fire was only 50 yards (15 m) away, one smokejumper named Wagner Dodge did something completely unexpected. He stopped running. Knowing that he couldn't outrun the fire, Dodge decided to try a tactic that hadn't been tried before. He would light a small escape fire in the path of the towering blaze.

As Dodge ignited the ground around him, he yelled at his men to stop running and join him. Then he wet his handkerchief with water from his canteen, clutched the cloth to his mouth, and hugged the smoldering ground he had just burned. As the fuel-hungry fire roared past him, Dodge tried to inhale the thin layer of oxygen that clung close to the ground. At times, the winds rushing past Dodge were so powerful that he was lifted right off of the ground.

Not only did Dodge's surprising and unexpected tactic end up saving his life, but it changed firefighting. After the Man Gulch fire, smokejumpers and other wild land firefighters were trained on escape fire tactics. In addition to escape fire tactics, wild land firefighters today are trained on using ultra-light and easy-to-deploy fireproof shelters that were developed thanks to technological advancements.

# French Fire Words

Laughing, Yow said, "So what happens to us if we aren't home by midnight? Do we turn into mice or pumpkins, or do we lose a shoe?"

Zenaida, the friend Yow was visiting, explained, "There's a town curfew for all teenagers. Unless accompanied by an adult, teenagers have to be off the street by 10:00 P.M. on school nights and by midnight on weekends."

"That's preposterous!" Yow said. "Isn't that a violation of our civil rights? This is a free country, so we shouldn't be prohibited from using public streets or spaces."

Jonathon, Zenaida's friend, added, "The curfew was voted on and accepted by the majority of the town council, a publicly elected body. It wasn't passed to create disharmony; it was only passed to keep teenagers safe."

Having finished his 48-hour shift, Mr. Montgomery, Zenaida's father and a city firefighter, happened to overhear Jonathon's comment as he walked in the door. He said, "Did you know that the word *curfew* has medieval French origins? In medieval France, the *courvre-feu* or 'cover-fire' was the hour when all the fires in town had to be put out, or at least covered, so people could sleep without fear. Over time, the word metamorphosed into the English 'curfew,' which means the time one needs to be back home or off the streets."

Maggie, an aspiring firefighter and Zenaida's older sister, said, "You can hear French in a word related to firefighting today. Firefighters have to practice *defenestrating* themselves because sometimes in life-or-death situations defenestration is necessary."

"What in the world does *defenestration* mean?" Yow asked.

Maggie replied, "In French, the word for 'window' is *fenetre.* When something is defenestrated, it is thrown out of a window. 'Defenestration' means throwing a person or a thing out of a window."

# Show What You Know

*The following are questions based on the passages "A Lifesaving Fire" and "French Fire Words." If needed, you may look back at the passages to answer the questions.*

1. **One reason Dodge did not deploy a fireproof shelter might be that**

   Ⓐ the fire was moving too quickly.

   Ⓑ he thought he could outrun the fire.

   Ⓒ the shelters had not yet been developed.

   Ⓓ it was in the gear the running firefighters dropped.

2. **One can tell that Yow could be visiting on a**

   Ⓐ Monday.

   Ⓑ Tuesday.

   Ⓒ Thursday.

   Ⓓ Saturday.

3. **What do both stories have in common?**

   Ⓐ fuel-hungry fires

   Ⓑ words with French origins

   Ⓒ an established safety curfew

   Ⓓ lifesaving firefighting tactics

4. **Smokejumpers today would most likely have less practice doing what than city firefighters?**

   Ⓐ defenestrating themselves.

   Ⓑ prohibiting an elected curfew.

   Ⓒ deploying a fireproof shelter.

   Ⓓ parachuting out of an airplane.

5. **From the stories, one can tell that**

   Ⓐ words from one language may have ties to another.

   Ⓑ French firefighters were the first to pass curfews.

   Ⓒ Maggie is aspiring to be a specialized smokejumper.

   Ⓓ not all firefighters train for life or death situations.

# Show What You Know (cont.)

6. **List the steps in order of what Dodge did to stay alive.**

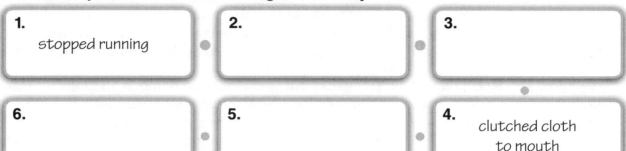

| | | |
|---|---|---|
| **1.** stopped running | **2.** | **3.** |
| **6.** | **5.** | **4.** clutched cloth to mouth |

7. **In the center box, write the name of the character in the story "French Fire Words" who is used as a reference point for all the other characters. In the remaining boxes, write in the names of the other characters and how they are related to the central character.**

Write three or four sentences that tell what each story is about.

8. **"A Lifesaving Fire"**

_____

_____

_____

9. **"French Fire Words"**

_____

_____

_____

10. **Take a side: Do you think towns or cities should be allowed to enact curfews for teenagers? Outline and defend your position. You may want to include in your defense a brief description of the history of the word "curfew" to help make your point.** *(Use a separate piece of paper. Your writing should be a few paragraphs long.)*

# The Longest Name

The place with the longest name in the world is in the country of Thailand. Thailand lies in the heart of Southeast Asia. It is bordered by Myanmar to the north and Laos to the northeast. Cambodia borders it to the southeast and Malaysia to the extreme south.

We know Thailand's capital as "Bangkok," but Bangkok's full name is 153 letters! Here it is: *Krungthepmahanakhonbowornvatanakosinmahintaraudyamahadilokpopnoparatanarajth aniburimudomrajniwesonahasatarnamornpimarnavatarsartitsakattiyavisanukamprasit.* Translated, this means, "city of angels, great city of immortals, magnificent jeweled city of the god Indra, seat of the king of Ayutthaya, city of gleaming temples, city of the king's most excellent palace and dominions, home of Vishnu and all the gods."

Bangkok is sometimes called the "Venice of the East" because, like Venice, Italy, Bangkok has a large number of canals. About 10,000 vendors travel in boats along the canals to make up the "Floating Market." From their boats, venders sell vegetables, fruit, dried fish, rice, flowers, and other products, as well as ready-to-eat food that they cooked on their floating kitchens. Traffic jams are often created due to the large number of boats, and special policemen traveling in their own boats try to keep the passageways clear.

Elephants were once very important in Thailand. Kings rode them into battle, and white, albino, and pinkish elephants were especially revered. Elephants were used for land transportation, as well as to help loggers deep in the forest. Although the importance of elephants in present-day Thailand has decreased, they are still used for taking tourists on rides in the jungle.

A popular game played in Bangkok and all over Thailand is *takraw*. Takraw, like volleyball, involves hitting a ball over a net—but in takraw, the ball cannot be touched by a player's hands! Instead, players have to get the ball over the net using their feet, heads, elbows, and knees.

# A Folktale from Thailand

A selfish king in Thailand once announced a contest. To receive a large lump of gold and the hand of the king's daughter in marriage, a man would only have to tell a story that was a lie, the verdict resting on the king's four counselors. This might seem an easy task, but no matter how preposterous the story was, the four counselors would always say, "Yes, this story could be true."

One day a simple farmer arrived at the court, stood before the king, and said, "Long, long ago, a boy tried to catch five elephants so he could ride them. The elephants fled from the boy, and the boy gave chase. He chased the magnificent creatures over mountains, rivers, lakes, and fields. As preposterous as it sounds, he even chased them up trees and across the ocean bottom! Somehow, whenever the boy came close, the elephants managed to escape.

"All this chasing took time, and the boy grew to be an elderly man who could no longer walk. The elderly man asked his son to continue the chase. I am that elderly man's son, now grown, and I caught the elephants a few years past. When I caught the elephants, I rode them into this very city, where I met four very wise counselors, the very four who will issue the verdict on my story today!

"Those four counselors were so impressed by my magnificent elephants that they wanted to purchase them. The price of the elephants was so high that the counselors promised to pay me at a later date. The date they agreed to is today. If the counselors and king agree that my story is true, please pay the money you owe to me. If it's false, bring out my reward and the princess!"

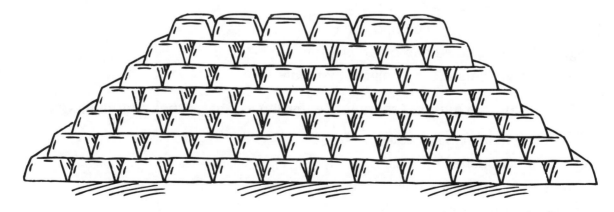

# Show What You Know

*The following are questions based on "The Longest Name" and "A Folktale from Thailand."*
*If needed, you may look back at the passages to answer the questions.*

1. **What phrase does not come from the translation of the capital of Bangkok's name?**

   Ⓐ great city of immortals

   Ⓑ city of gleaming temples

   Ⓒ city of Indra's floating market

   Ⓓ city of the king's most excellent palace and dominions

2. **When something is preposterous, it is**

   Ⓐ so clearly wrong it is laughable.

   Ⓑ so impressive it deserves a reward.

   Ⓒ so great it is simply magnificent.

   Ⓓ so expensive it cannot be paid immediately.

3. **What do both stories have in common?**

   Ⓐ an animal revered in Thailand

   Ⓑ a game played all over Thailand

   Ⓒ a market in Thailand where elephants are sold

   Ⓓ a story about how Thailand's capital was named

4. **From the stories, one can tell that most likely**

   Ⓐ elephants are used in takraw.

   Ⓑ Thailand has or once had a king.

   Ⓒ only a king could ride on an elephant.

   Ⓓ more vendors are in Thailand than Italy.

5. **When judging a game of takraw, the verdict might be that a hit is illegal if**

   Ⓐ a knee touches the ball.

   Ⓑ a hand touches the ball.

   Ⓒ a foot touches the ball.

   Ⓓ an elbow touches the ball.

# Show What You Know *(cont.)*

6. **Using information from the story and the labeled map to the right, fill in the names of the countries that border Thailand.**

   *Country A:* _____

   *Country B:* _____

   *Country C:* _____

   *Country D:* _____

7. **Fill in the chart with information about the elements of "A Folktale from Thailand."**

| Action | farmer tells story about selling elephants to counselors |
|---|---|
| Characters | |
| Setting | |
| Problem | |
| Result | |

**Write three or four sentences that tell what each story is about.**

8. **"The Longest Name"**

   _____

   _____

   _____

9. **"A Folktale from Thailand"**

   _____

   _____

   _____

10. **Think of a city name. The name can belong to any city that you want. Then, think up a preposterous tale about how this city was so named or what the name means. Your explanation should include such story elements as characters, setting, problem, action, and result.** *(Use a separate piece of paper. Your writing should be a few paragraphs long.)*

# Why Spider-Man Isn't Mosquito-Man

Just one man created many of the comic-book heroes we are familiar with today. This celebrated comic-book author's name is Stan Lee. Lee's real name was "Stanley Leiber," but his byline is "Stan Lee." Lee chose his byline in 1941 when he was first published. Lee said later that the reason he wrote under a byline was that he felt that one day he'd be writing the "Great American Novel," and he didn't want to use his real name on "silly little comics."

Lee found that many people didn't consider his comics silly at all. Readers considered them fun, entertaining, thrilling, and imaginative, and they bought them in large numbers. One reason the industry became so large was because of Lee's innovative characters. Among Lee's new and changed characters were Mr. Fantastic, the Invisible Girl, the Human Torch, and the Thing (all of the Fantastic Four). Lee also created the Incredible Hulk, the Mighty Thor, Iron Man, Doctor Strange, Daredevil, and the X-Men.

**author Stan Lee**

Perhaps Lee's most famous character is Spider-Man. Lee said he was trying to think of an innovative and unique superpower for a superhero, but he was having trouble because there were already characters that were the strongest in the world, could fly, could turn invisible, etc. In the midst of his musings, Lee spotted a fly on the wall. Watching the fly led Lee to think about a superhero whose unique superpower could be the power to stick on a wall like an insect. Lee first thought of Mosquito-Man for a name, but he decided against it because it didn't have any glamour. He thought of Insect-Man, but he decided that was even worse. After running through several more names, Lee came up with a name that he felt sounded mysterious and dramatic: Spider-Man.

# With Great Power

When Jake's grandmother entered the living room and found Jake lying on the couch reading a comic book, she snapped, "Don't waste your time. You should be reading true literature, not that irresponsible drivel that can't teach you anything."

"Some comics may be nonsense, Grandma," Jake said, "but Spider-Man is someone I can relate to. Unlike other superheroes that perhaps came from different planets, Peter Parker, or Spider-Man, is more realistic. Instead of living in a fictitious city, he lives in New York City. Even though he has the relative strength of a spider, he has to rely on his acrobatic abilities and his homemade web-shooter."

Jake's grandmother couldn't help herself. She was interested. "So why does he have the relative strength of a spider?" she asked.

"Oh, Peter was bitten by a radioactive spider that had dangled in front of a laser beam when he was attending a science exhibit," Jake explained. "Peter developed the relative strength of a spider when the spider's venom entered his bloodstream."

"It may be interesting, but I contend it is drivel," Jake's grandmother said. "You should be reading speeches of great world leaders. Now, that would provide you with character development."

"Yes, I suppose that's true," said Jake, "because with great power, there must also come great responsibility."

"Exactly!" cried Jake's grandmother. "Was it Thomas Jefferson, Patrick Henry, or Abraham Lincoln who said that?"

"Um, Grandma," Jake replied, "It was Spider-Man. In the comic, we find out that Peter's beloved uncle was killed by a robber Peter had refused to stop earlier that day. Peter was grief-stricken, and he vowed from that moment on that he would never again pass up the chance to confront evil. That's when he developed his motto, 'With great power there must also come great responsibility.'"

# Show What You Know

*The following are questions based on the passages "Why Spider-Man Isn't Mosquito-Man" and "With Great Power." If needed, you may look back at the passages to answer the questions.*

1. **Stan Lee was an innovative writer because he created**

    (A) new characters.

    (B) fun characters.

    (C) thrilling characters.

    (D) mysterious characters.

2. **Why might Jake's grandmother agree that comic books aren't all drivel?**

    (A) They can be interesting.

    (B) They can be easy to relate to.

    (C) They can help develop one's character.

    (D) They can be about characters from real cities.

3. **What do both stories have in common?**

    (A) They both mention great speeches.

    (B) They both mention fictitious characters.

    (C) They both mention a writer with a byline.

    (D) They both mention how Spider-Man gained his powers.

4. **From the stories, one can tell that Stan Lee**

    (A) didn't care about character development.

    (B) didn't know how well his comic books would sell.

    (C) didn't think it important to read great literature.

    (D) didn't know that comics are more important than novels.

5. **Most likely Stan Lee**

    (A) had some characters with the same superpowers.

    (B) had other characters that used Spider-Man's motto.

    (C) had wanted to develop characters people could relate to.

    (D) had tried to write his "Great American Novel" before writing comic books.

# Show What You Know (cont.)

6. **Write down the first two adjectives, thoughts, or images that come to mind when you read the following names:**

*Mosquito-Man* _____bug_____         _____mail_____

*Insect-Man* _____         _____

*Fly-Man* _____         _____

*Lizard-Man* _____         _____

*Spider-Man* _____         _____

7. **Fill in the boxes to show the elements of "With Great Power."**

| Setting | Characters | Action/Problem | Outcome |
|---|---|---|---|
| Grandmas living room | Grandma Jake | Grandma hates comics | She likes comics |

**Write three or four sentences that tell what each story is about.**

8. **"Why Spider-Man Isn't Mosquito-Man"**

Stan Lee is ist thinking of creative comic book caroters, he sees a fly, and then he thinks of spider man.

9. **"With Great Power"**

Jakes Grandma hates comics. Jake explans why it is good liciadure Jakes grand ma is ok with commics.

10. **If you could be an existing superhero or have a special kind of superpower, who would you be or what power would you have? Write one paragraph explaining your answer. In a second paragraph, discuss Spider-Man's motto. Tell if you think why it should or shouldn't apply to you now that you have a superpower and how this might affect your life.** *(Use a separate piece of paper.)*

# On the Most Dangerous Lighthouse

The five men had been solid friends for years, but now they couldn't stand the sight of one another. The men hadn't spoken one word to each other for a month. When they ate, they faced away from each other or avoided the table and ate alone. As fistfights broke out and men threatened one another, each man tried to avoid all others to minimize the harm they were inflicting on each other.

The men were lighthouse keepers on St. George Lighthouse. St. George Lighthouse was located on a tiny, low spit of a rock six miles (9.7 km) off the northern California coast, with the closest port being Crescent City, 13 miles (20.8 km) away. It was built in 1892, and because it was too dangerous and expensive to maintain, it was replaced by a 42-foot-high (12.8 m) self-contained navigation aid in 1975.

Before 1975, lighthouse keepers had to be brought to St. George by boat, as did all food, water, fuel, and medical supplies. Once at the island, the men and supplies had to suffer through a dangerous stories-high, wind-swung ride as they were hoisted by hook from the churning sea up to the lighthouse.

At times, harsh weather meant that keepers were more isolated than usual. In 1937, when the five men stopped talking, they were confined to the rock for almost two full months. They were nearly out of food, water, and fuel, and hadn't been able to bathe or shave in over a month. Although the men found each other unbearable during the storm, their attitudes changed immediately after. As George Roux, the head lighthouse keeper, explained, "Funny thing, the moment the weather pressure let up, so did our pressures and we returned to normal, too. We were friends again. Talked our heads off."

# What Madeline Found Good

"I want you to welcome our new student Madeline," Mrs. Ballantyne told the class. "Her father is the new lighthouse keeper at Rochester Lighthouse. In the mornings, when the tide is low, she'll walk to school, but in the afternoons, when its high tide, her mother or her father will row a boat over to pick her up. When weather conditions make it too dangerous to pick her up, her parents have arranged for her to stay with the Schneider family."

As Madeline sat down, Mrs. Ballantyne asked her if she enjoyed living at the lighthouse. "It's wonderful!" Madeline exclaimed. "Rochester Lighthouse is very safe compared to St. George Lighthouse, where my father was previously stationed. Sometimes we wouldn't see him for months because conditions on St. George were so dangerous that families weren't allowed to live there or even visit.

"At Rochester Lighthouse, we can dock a boat and climb stairs up to the lighthouse. At St. George, all the supplies had to be ferried over by boat—but a boat couldn't dock! Getting up to the lighthouse was horribly dangerous, because the keepers and supplies had to be hoisted up by a derrick with ropes, pulleys, and a long boom that extended 60 feet over the ocean! Sometimes huge, 15-foot waves almost covered my father when he was being hoisted up!"

The students were so interested in what Madeline was saying that they didn't stop asking questions all day. They even followed her down to the water after school so that they could continue to question her until her father arrived. Once in the boat, Madeline didn't say a word. When they arrived at the lighthouse, she said, "It's so good to be home alone with only the sound of wind and waves for company."

# Show What You Know

*The following are questions based on "On the Most Dangerous Lighthouse" and "What Madeline Found Good." If needed, you may look back at the passages to answer the questions.*

1. **When something is isolated, it is**

   Ⓐ hoisted.
   Ⓑ set apart.
   Ⓒ dangerous.
   Ⓓ minimizing harm.

2. **Madeline might**

   Ⓐ row with her father to school.
   Ⓑ row with her mother home from school.
   Ⓒ walk with her mother home from school.
   Ⓓ walk with her father home from school.

3. **What do both stories have in common?**

   Ⓐ details about an expensive-to-maintain lighthouse
   Ⓑ details about almost running out of food and water
   Ⓒ details about a self-contained navigational device
   Ⓓ details about being hoisted up to Rochester Lighthouse

4. **What is not true about getting on and off St. George Lighthouse?**

   Ⓐ It was a dangerous wind-swung ride.
   Ⓑ A derrick with ropes and pulleys was used.
   Ⓒ The derrick's boom extended out over the ocean.
   Ⓓ Men and supplies were hoisted from a docked boat.

5. **What year could Madeline's father have been stationed at St. George Lighthouse?**

   Ⓐ 1785
   Ⓑ 1875
   Ⓒ 1911
   Ⓓ 2002

# Show What You Know (cont.)

6. Fill in how the men at St. George Lighthouse felt about each other.

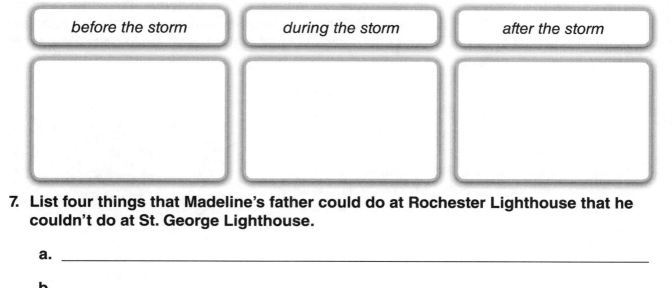

| before the storm | during the storm | after the storm |
|---|---|---|
|  |  |  |

7. List four things that Madeline's father could do at Rochester Lighthouse that he couldn't do at St. George Lighthouse.

   a. _____

   b. _____

   c. _____

   d. _____

Write three or four sentences that tell what each story is about.

8. "On the Most Dangerous Lighthouse"

_____

_____

_____

9. "What Madeline Found Good"

_____

_____

_____

10. If you were stationed at a lighthouse, would you rather it be St. George Lighthouse or Rochester Lighthouse? Explain your answer, making sure to mention details from the story about the lighthouses. *(Use a separate piece of paper. Your writing should be a few paragraphs long.)*

# Fascinating Body Facts

The muscular system is one of 10 systems found in the human body. The other systems are the nervous, skeletal, circulatory, respiratory, digestive, excretory, immune, endocrine, and reproductive systems. About 660 muscles, most of them working in pairs, help to make up the muscular system.

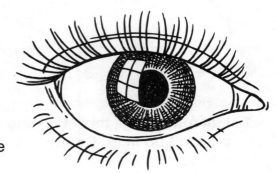

Some of the most active muscles in your body are not the ones that help you walk or throw a ball. They are not the 42 muscles that you use to frown or the 17 muscles you use to smile. Some of the most active muscles are the eye muscles. These muscles contract, tightening and becoming shorter, about 100,000 times a day. These muscles are very active when you are sleeping, because then your eye muscles move around while you dream.

The human heart is a muscle that, along with your blood vessels and blood, makes up the circulatory system. About the size of a fist, the heart acts like a powerful pump. Never resting, it circulates blood throughout your body about three times every minute. An infant's heart beats on average about 130 times a minute. A mature adult's heart beats on average about 70 times per minute. (Contrast this to an elephant's heart, which on average beats only about 25 times a minute!)

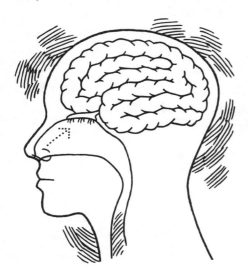

Breathing involves the respiratory system. When one breathes, the lungs take in oxygen from the air. Many people think that we take in a breath every time our heart beats. This is erroneous, as the number of breaths we take depends on our level of activity. A resting child may take only 30 breaths a minute, but if he or she begins to exercise strenuously, the figure may go up to 60.

# Body Math

"Are you ready for the first Body Math Tournament question?" Ms. Thundercloud queried her students.

"Yes," replied the excited students, answering in unison.

Ms. Thundercloud smiled, nodded approvingly at her class, and then proceeded to ask the first question. "As you mature," she said, "what body part decreases from 300 to 206 individual pieces?"

First to raise her hand, Daphne answered, "Newborn babies have 300 bones in their bodies, but as they grow, some of the bones fuse together, and that's why we end up with 94 fewer bones than we started with."

Ms. Thundercloud's next query was, "What inside your body, if laid out end-to-end, would measure more than 59,000 miles (94,500 km)?"

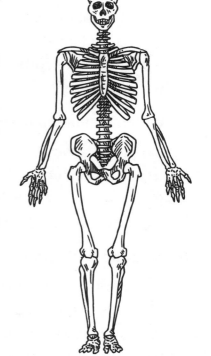

Chung Sook was able to answer before anyone else. He said, "All of our blood vessels, including the arteries that carry oxygen-rich blood away from our hearts and our veins that carry oxygen-depleted blood back to our hearts, if laid out end-to-end would measure a distance more than twice Earth's circumference."

"Correct," Ms. Thundercloud told Chung Sook. "If all of our blood vessels were laid out end-to-end, they could stretch more than twice around the Earth. Now, speaking of large amounts, what do scientists estimate adults have 75 trillion of?"

Braden answered quickly, "Scientists estimate that adults have 75 trillion cells. Not all the cells are the same. Blood cells, skin cells, and nerve cells are just a few examples of the different types of cells that make up our body."

"And which type of cell type is it," asked Ms. Thundercloud, "that makes up a large part of household dust?"

"Most of the dust is made up of flakes of dead skin" cried out Stephanie and Alan in unison, "because the dead cells are constantly being worn away."

# Show What You Know

*The following are questions based on the passages "Fascinating Body Facts" and "Body Math." If needed, you may look back at the passages to answer the questions.*

1. **In the story "Fascinating Body Facts," the least amount of information was provided on the**

   Ⓐ skeletal system.

   Ⓑ muscular system.

   Ⓒ respiratory system.

   Ⓓ circulatory system.

2. **Which statement is true about the human body?**

   Ⓐ It has about 75 trillion cells.

   Ⓑ It has about 75 trillion skin cells.

   Ⓒ It has about 75 trillion blood vessel cells.

   Ⓓ It has about 75 trillion different cell types.

3. **What do both stories have in common?**

   Ⓐ queries about the body

   Ⓑ facts about the body's circumference

   Ⓒ answers about the body's most active system

   Ⓓ information about parts of the body's systems

4. **From the stories, one can tell that one's**

   Ⓐ heart is not part of the circulatory system.

   Ⓑ lungs are not part of the circulatory system.

   Ⓒ veins are not part of the circulatory system.

   Ⓓ arteries are not part of the circulatory system.

5. **From the stories, one can tell that**

   Ⓐ bodies do not change as they mature.

   Ⓑ one uses more muscles to frown than to smile.

   Ⓒ a breath is taken every time the heart contracts.

   Ⓓ some infant bones flake off as they are worn away.

# Show What You Know (cont.)

6. **Write down the fact from the story "Fascinating Body Facts" that goes with each number.**

3 _____     60 _____

10 _____     70 _____

17 _____     130 _____

30 _____     660 _____

42 _____     100,000 _____

7. **Fill in the chart with information from the story "Body Math."**

| Question # | 1 | 2 | 3 | 4 |
|---|---|---|---|---|
| Answer | | | | |
| Who Answered | | | | |

**Write three or four sentences that tell what each story is about.**

8. **"Fascinating Body Facts"**

_____

_____

_____

9. **"Body Math"**

_____

_____

_____

10. **Use information from the story "Fascinating Body Facts" to add to the story "Body Math." Your addition to the story should include two or more questions. Remember to use quotation marks around direct quotes.** *(Use a separate piece of paper. Your writing should be a few paragraphs long.)*

# Hero in the Storm

On July 6, 1881, a deadly storm raged across the Iowa countryside. Fifteen-year-old Kate Shelley knew something was horribly wrong. Well past 11 o'clock at night, she had heard a pusher engine on the nearby railroad track clang its bell twice. Then she had heard the sound of a dreadful crash and the awful hiss of steam as hot metal hit cold water.

Despite the fierce winds and torrential rain, Kate knew she had to try to help. With lantern in hand, she ran to where she had heard the crash. She found the bridge out, the engine in the water, and two men hanging onto branches, desperately trying to stop themselves from being swept away in the thundering water.

Kate was unable to reach the men, and even worse, Kate knew that a passenger train with hundreds of passengers was due in an hour. Without hesitating, Kate turned into the pelting rain and raced for a telegraph station across another bridge in the opposite direction.

When Kate reached the bridge, her terror mounted. The wind had long extinguished her lantern's feeble flame, and the bridge, nearly 700 feet (213 m) long, was a ladder of cross ties, each nearly two feet (61 cm) apart. In addition, the splintery ties of the bridge were studded with twisted spikes and nails to discourage foot traffic.

Despite her fears that the oncoming passenger train would run her over and of falling into the raging water splashing up below, Kate crawled on hands and knees across the bridge. Using her fingers to locate the next tie, Kate ignored her bleeding hands and knees and thought only of saving lives. Finally reaching solid ground, Kate raced to the station where she warned the men there of the impending danger.

# An End to the Story

"I'm not satisfied," Derrick said in a disgruntled voice.

"What do you find so dissatisfying?" asked Mr. Chopra.

"It was a good story about Kate Shelley," Derrick replied, "it being nonfiction and all, but I found the ending disgruntling because I would like to know if Kate got to the station in time to stop the oncoming passenger train. It really isn't clear."

"Would it make her less of a hero?" wondered Trang.

"No, it wouldn't make her less of a hero, because Kate went as fast as she could and put herself in extreme danger, but I would just prefer a conclusion that was more informative," Derrick replied.

Nodding, Mr. Chopra told his class, "Extra points to anyone who can come up with a more complete conclusion. Sources could be books or old newspaper clippings. You might check out the library or reputable sites on the Internet."

The next morning, hands waved in the air when Mr. Chopra asked if anyone had found out something. Lillian went first: "I found several articles about Kate's heroics in various newspapers archived on the Internet. It ends up that she was in no risk of being run over by the passenger train while she crossed the bridge because the train had been halted 40 miles (64 km) to the west because of the storm."

"That concurs with the information in a book by Robert San Souci that I found in the library," Kareem said. "San Souci describes how, despite her exhaustion, Kate braved the storm again, leading the men at the station to the two men stranded in the floodwaters from the pusher-engine crash. Those two men survived only because of Kate's fortitude and amazing bravery."

"I'm satisfied with that story ending," Derrick said, his voice free of disgruntlement.

# Show What You Know

*The following are questions based on the passages "Hero in the Storm" and "An End to the Story." If needed, you may look back at the passages to answer the questions.*

1. **What statement is not true about the bridge Kate crossed?**

   (A) It was a ladder of cross ties.

   (B) It had a section for foot traffic.

   (C) It was nearly 700 feet (213 m) long.

   (D) Its ties were studded with twisted spikes and nails.

2. **Who used a book as a source?**

   (A) Trang

   (B) Kareem

   (C) Robert

   (D) Lillian

3. **What do both stories have in common?**

   (A) They are both about an event that happened in 1882.

   (B) They are both about researching a crash.

   (C) They are both about a satisfactory ending.

   (D) They are both about a 15-year-old hero from Iowa.

4. **What must be true about Kate Shelley?**

   (A) She could see fairly well in the dark.

   (B) She knew the men from the pusher engine would survive.

   (C) She was familiar with the times the trains ran past her house.

   (D) She wouldn't have crossed the bridge if she had known the passenger train had been stopped.

5. **What word seems the most unlikely fit when describing Kate Shelley?**

   (A) strong

   (B) determined

   (C) courageous

   (D) disgruntled

# Show What You Know (cont.)

6. **Fill in the boxes with information about Kate from the story "Hero in the Storm" in the order that it happened.**

**1.** *hears engine bell*

**2.**

**3.**

**4.** *finds men in water*

**5.**

**6.**

7. **Use information from the story "An End to the Story" to fill in one final box about what Kate did.**

**7.**

**Write three or four sentences that tell what each story is about.**

8. **"Hero in the Storm"**

_____

_____

_____

9. **"An End to the Story"**

_____

_____

_____

10. **Think of a story where you found yourself disgruntled at its conclusion. The story may be historical or present-day, fiction or nonfiction. It may come from a book, newspaper, television, movie, or even something you overheard. In one paragraph, very briefly describe the story and its conclusion. In a second paragraph, tell why the conclusion was not satisfactory to you and what might have been added or changed to make it more pleasing.** *(Use a separate piece of paper.)*

# Scorpion Scientist

Gary Polis knelt down one dark night in a desert sand dune in Southern California. He felt something soft and squishy under his knee. Polis, a biologist, was studying scorpions in their natural habitat. Scorpions are most active at night, but Polis was able to conduct his research using ultraviolet (UV) light. Scorpions glow under UV light, but it doesn't harm or bother them. Scorpion eyes are most sensitive to low levels of light, and scorpions can navigate using shadows cast by starlight.

Knowing that anything soft and squishy was most likely a sidewinder rattlesnake, Polis jumped back immediately. Sidewinders, like all rattlesnakes, are venomous vipers. Unlike scorpions, rattlesnakes do not glow under UV light. Although Polis was not bitten by the snake, he did not escape from harm. When Polis jumped back, he landed on a cactus and ended up with 38 cactus spines in his backside.

To prevent further injury from surprise snake encounters, Polis did two things. First, he caught some of the rattlesnakes in the vicinity and sprayed them with paint that glowed under UV light. Second, he began to wear special snake chaps that were made of woven brass metal.

Over the years, Polis has studied many different species of scorpions around the world. (There are about 1,500 known scorpion species, with only about 25 species venomous enough to kill a human.) One scorpion Polis studied ended up being a record holder. The scorpion lived along the high-tide mark on the beaches of the Mexican peninsula of Baja California. Its record was for population density. Polis found that two to a dozen of these scorpions lived within any square meter of shore habitat. As Polis remarked, "It is not a good place to spread your sleeping bag."

# Scorpion Charlatan

"These venomous scorpions have not been fed for over a week! Still, ladies and gentlemen, the Amazing Master of the Scorpions, Sir Apollo Sting, will, while showing no fear or trepidation, put 12—yes, a dozen—of the largest and most colossal of these dangerous beasts on his face! Yes, ladies and gentleman, you did hear me correctly! Sir Apollo Sting's amazing performance will terrorize and astonish, horrify and fascinate, repulse and amaze! Just five dollars earns you entry way into the tent and witness to the only man in the world who is brave enough to perform such a dangerous feat!"

Kaitlyn listened to the hawker, who was dressed in his fancy jacket and top hat outside the circus tent, and said, "Adrianna, this is worth paying for. Imagine, a man putting venomous creatures on his face!"

Adrianna said, "I'm sure the man's a charlatan, a trickster. But if you want to waste your money, then so be it."

As Kaitlyn paid the hawker she said to Adrianna, "I just know Apollo isn't a charlatan. His act won't be a trick at all."

As Kaitlyn and Adrianna watched Apollo Sting place a dozen scorpions on his face, Kaitlyn whispered, "Look at the size of those scorpions' claws! They're huge! This isn't a fake act at all. There's a man in front of us covered with a dozen hungry, venomous creatures!"

Adrianna said, "Despite appearances, Apollo isn't in great danger."

"How can you say that?" Kaitlyn demanded.

"First," answered Adrianna, "Scorpions can go a year without eating, as they have some of the lowest rates of animal metabolism ever recorded. Scorpions have lower metabolisms than growing carrot or radish roots! Second, scorpions with large claws rely mostly on their claws for food getting and have venom no worse than a bee sting."

# Show What You Know

*The following are questions based on the passages "Scorpion Scientist" and "Scorpion Charlatan." If needed, you may look back at the passages to answer the questions.*

1. **Which statement is true?**

   Ⓐ All rattlesnakes are sidewinders.
   Ⓑ Some sidewinders are rattlesnakes.
   Ⓒ Most sidewinders are rattlesnakes.
   Ⓓ Some rattlesnakes are sidewinders.

2. **The hawker did not say that one would feel _____ if one watched Apollo Sting.**

   Ⓐ horror
   Ⓑ repulsion.
   Ⓒ trepidation.
   Ⓓ astonishment.

3. **What do both stories have in common?**

   Ⓐ a venomous viper
   Ⓑ a venomous species
   Ⓒ a venomous metabolism
   Ⓓ a venomous record-holder

4. **What would make Polis a charlatan?**

   Ⓐ only pretending to conduct research
   Ⓑ dressing in a fancy jacket and top hat
   Ⓒ studying only scorpions with large claws
   Ⓓ covering his face with a dozen venomous creatures

5. **What does one know about the scorpions Apollo put on his face?**

   Ⓐ They glow under UV light.
   Ⓑ Their natural habitat is the desert.
   Ⓒ They are among the 25 most venomous.
   Ⓓ Their population density increases when they are fed.

# Show What You Know *(cont.)*

6. **List the two things Polis did to prevent further injury from surprise snake encounters.**

    a. _____

    b. _____

7. **On the longer line, write down who said what in the story. Then, on the shorter line, list in order when it was said. Use the numbers 1 to 5. Put "1" by what happened first. Put "5" by what happened last.**

    _____ "I'm sure the man's a charlatan..."                     _____

    _____ "Scorpions have lower metabolisms
    than growing carrot radish roots."                           _____

    _____ "How can you say that?"                                 _____

    _____ "Look at the size of those scorpions' claws!"          _____

    _____ "Yes, ladies and gentlemen, you did hear me correctly."  _____

**Write three or four sentences that tell what each story is about.**

8. **"Scorpion Scientist"**

    _____

    _____

    _____

9. **"Scorpion Charlatan"**

    _____

    _____

    _____

10. **Write what you might say if you were a hawker trying to get people to pay to enter a tent where they can view scorpions. Use facts from both stories in your writing. You may want to review the first paragraph in "Scorpion Charlatan" before you start writing. Note that every sentence in this paragraph ends in an exclamation point.** *(Use a separate piece of paper. Your writing should be a few paragraphs long.)*

# Why the Doctor Shocked

A doctor for the Union Army during the Civil War, Walker wore the Union officer's blue uniform. Pants with gold stripes were part of the uniform, as was a bright green surgeon's sash that was worn about the waist. After the war, Walker was awarded with the Congressional Medal of Honor. The Congressional Medal of Honor is the nation's highest award for valor, and it was Walker's most cherished possession. Walker wore this medal, pinned to a men's suit jacket lapel, whenever in public. If Walker was a surgeon and presented with the nation's highest award for valor, why were people shocked at what Walker wore?

**Dr. Mary Edwards Walker**

Walker was a woman. Instead of wearing the long dresses and tight corsets that were popular at the time, Dr. Mary Edwards Walker wore men's suits. Walker believed in dress reform. She felt that women's fashions were cumbersome, unsanitary, and dangerous. They were cumbersome (hard to handle and unwieldy) because of the weight of the many yards of fabric that went into just one garment. They were unsanitary because they swept the floor like a broom and collected grime. They were dangerous because the tightly laced corsets made it difficult for a woman to breathe and displaced their internal organs.

Walker was a selfless doctor. Several times, when other army doctors refused to cross into Confederate territory for fear of being captured, Walker would go alone to care for the wounded. On April 10, 1864, while on one mission, Walker was captured. She was placed behind bars in a filthy Confederate prison. At night, Walker had to sleep on an insect-infested mattress. She could hear rats and other vermin boldly scurry across the dirty floors. Walker remained in prison until August, when she was released in a prisoner exchange.

# An Even Trade for Style

With exasperation, Katrina said, "I wish I had a magic wand. I'd wave it over my head so my hair would look desirable, fashionable, and stylish. I've spent uncomfortable hours highlighting and curling, and all for something that will last only a day."

Odessa, Katrina's friend and schoolmate, said, "There's a history connection between wands and hair."

As Han-Ling, another of Katrina's friend's, carefully tied up her hair, she asked, "How can there be a historical connection between wands and hair?"

Odessa explained, "During the latter part of the 1700s, French women styled their hair in high, towering headdresses that took hours to style and cost a lot but lasted for weeks."

"Sounds like an even trade," Katrina commented while continuing to primp.

"Not so fast," answered Odessa. "To keep one's hair from harm, one had to duck under doorways and sleep sitting up. Did you know that during that time, carriages had to be made with higher roofs?"

Laughing, Han-Ling queried, "But where do the wands come in?"

"Oh," Odessa explained, "the headdresses were constructed with wire frames, cotton padding, and switches of horsehair. They were coated with sticky cream, powdered with starch, and decorated with jewels and feathers. Vermin, including lice, bugs, and sometimes even mice, would take up residence in the women's hair. The women carried wands so they could slide the wands into their hair and scratch their heads without disturbing their headdresses."

As Katrina and Han-Ling burst out with cries of repulsion and disgust, they put down their brushes, barrettes, and curling and straightening irons and made their way to the door.

"Careful," warned Odessa. "We don't want to jostle each other or go too fast. With our platform shoes and high heels it would be all too easy to fall and break an ankle."

# Show What You Know

*The following are questions based on the passages "Why the Doctor Shocked" and "An Even Trade for Style." If needed, you may look back at the passages to answer the questions.*

1. **In what part of the story "Why the Doctor Shocked" does one first learn that Walker is a woman?**

    Ⓐ the title
    Ⓑ first paragraph
    Ⓒ second paragraph
    Ⓓ third paragraph

2. **What does one know about Katrina's hairstyle?**

    Ⓐ It had curls.
    Ⓑ It made her feel repulsion.
    Ⓒ It used switches of horsehair.
    Ⓓ It lasted as long as a French headdress.

3. **What do both stories have in common?**

    Ⓐ the history of dress reform
    Ⓑ a discussion on hairstyles
    Ⓒ details about what doctors wore
    Ⓓ information about women's fashions

4. **When Walker heard vermin,**

    Ⓐ it could have only been rats.
    Ⓑ she knew she would be released.
    Ⓒ it might have been mice or small bugs.
    Ⓓ she needed a wand to slide into her hair.

5. **How would Walker most likely feel about the shoes Katrina, Han-Ling, and Odessa were wearing?**

    Ⓐ that they were dangerous
    Ⓑ that they were desirable
    Ⓒ that they were unsanitary
    Ⓑ that they were too tightly laced

58

# Show What You Know (cont.)

6. **Write down three things Walker felt about women's fashions and why.**

   a. _____

   _____

   b. _____

   _____

   c. _____

   _____

7. **Write down in order who spoke in the story "An Even Trade for Style."**

| 1. | 2. | 3. | 4. |
|---|---|---|---|

| 8. | 7. | 6. | 5. |
|---|---|---|---|

**Write three or four sentences that tell what each story is about.**

8. **"Why the Doctor Shocked"**

   _____

   _____

   _____

9. **"An Even Trade for Style"**

   _____

   _____

   _____

10. **On a separate piece of paper, write one or two paragraphs about fashion where you do the following:**

   ✣ *describe something you like or don't like (think of types of clothing, hair styles, brand names, piercings, tattoos, etc.)*

   ✣ *explain if this style is practical or unsafe.*

# Who Dialed 911?

Chris Trott, the dispatcher for the Scottsdale, Arizona, 911 emergency call center, tried repeatedly to get a response. "Hello, this is 911. Hello? Can you hear me? Is there somebody there you can give the phone to?" he said. Despite Trott's repeated queries to whomever had dialed 911, no one answered. All Trott could hear was a dog whimpering and barking.

When Trott alerted the police, officers were dispatched immediately to the location of the call. When the officers arrived, they could hear a dog barking loudly inside the house. Once inside, they found the dog's owner incapacitated and in dire need of medical care. The dog's owner was a man named Joe Stainaker. Stainaker hadn't been able to call 911 because he had suffered a massive seizure.

It was Buddy, an 18-month-old German shepherd, who had contacted 911. Buddy was Stainaker's trained assistance dog. Stainaker needed an assistance dog because he suffered from seizures that could come on at any time and without warning. (The seizures were due to a head injury Stainaker had suffered 10 years before.) As some of the bigger and more massive seizures left Stainaker in an incapacitated state and unable to call 911, Stainaker had trained Buddy to press programmed buttons until a 911 operator came on the line and responded.

Scottsdale Police Sgt. Mark Clark said that it wasn't the first time Buddy had saved Stainaker's life. Clark explained that police are always dispatched to a 911 call, but that Stainaker's address was flagged in the Scottsdale emergency notification system. It was flagged that a trained assistance dog could call 911 when the owner was incapacitated. Clark said that two times previously, Buddy had contacted 911 when Stainaker was in need.

# Overlooked Heroes

As David threw his ball for Princess, his golden retriever, he said to his friend Danielle, "The majority of pet owners in the United States have cats, and I'm perplexed as to why. Dogs can protect us, fetch, pull sleds, and help us hunt. What can a domesticated cat do better than a domesticated dog?"

Danielle said, "David, domesticated cats are overlooked American heroes!"

When David snorted, Danielle said, "Listen and learn, my friend. First of all, without domesticated cats, the early American colonies would have been overrun with rats. In the 1740s, Pennsylvania was besieged by a rodent epidemic so large that they had to import cats! Think, too, of the early farmers in the Midwest who needed cats to keep rats, mice, and other rodents from eating their crops and stored seeds."

When Princess ran up, dropping her ball at David's feet so that he could throw it for her again, Danielle said, "Princess's golden coat reminds me of the California gold rush. One entrepreneur purchased about 100 cats for 10 cents apiece and paid to ship them to San Francisco. There, he sold them for $20 dollars each to the miners. Why were the miners so willing to purchase such expensive felines? They needed good mousers to keep rats from biting them at night! I'm telling you, David, that was one businessman whose entrepreneurship resulted in a profit worth purring about!

"One last thing," continued Danielle. "The famous American author Mark Twain gave his cats difficult names to say—like Blatherskite, for example—so that his children would learn how to pronounce hard words."

"Cats are useful," David conceded, "but not smart enough to know that a blatherskite is a blustering, talkative fellow."

"A dog wouldn't know that either," Danielle quickly pointed out.

# Show What You Know

*The following are questions based on the passages "Who Dialed 911?" and "Overlooked Heroes." If needed, you may look back at the passages to answer the questions.*

1. **If one is incapacitated,**

    Ⓐ one is flagged.

    Ⓑ one is unable to help oneself.

    Ⓒ one is programmed.

    Ⓓ one is dispatched.

2. **To find out the entrepreneur's true profit on each cat, one would have to subtract the price of shipping each cat to San Francisco from**

    Ⓐ $19.10

    Ⓑ $19.90

    Ⓒ $20.00

    Ⓓ $20.10

3. **What are both stories about?**

    Ⓐ helpful domestic animals

    Ⓑ animals that need assistance

    Ⓒ profits to be made on animals

    Ⓓ what we can learn from animals

4. **From the stories, one can tell that**

    Ⓐ no cats can push buttons.

    Ⓑ all dogs know how to call 911.

    Ⓒ some dog names are hard to pronounce.

    Ⓓ both cats and dogs can be of assistance.

5. **Mark Clark would not appear to be a blatherskite because**

    Ⓐ he wasn't a feline.

    Ⓑ he could say hard-to-pronounce names.

    Ⓒ he was a police sergeant in Scottsdale, Arizona.

    Ⓓ he didn't take credit for saving Stainaker's life.

# Show What You Know *(cont.)*

6.  **Keep the characters straight! Write down the full names of the characters from the story "Who Dialed 911?" in each box. Jot down one or two details about each character below their name.**

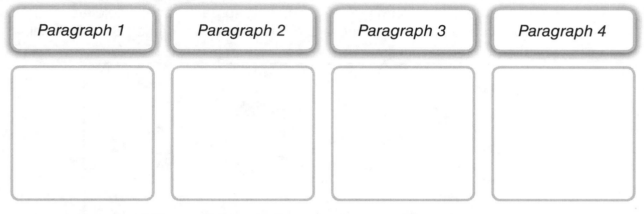

| Paragraph 1 | Paragraph 2 | Paragraph 3 | Paragraph 4 |

7.  **List three examples Danielle used to show that cats can assist people.**

    a. _____

    b. _____

    c. _____

**Write three or four sentences that tell what each story is about.**

8.  **"Who Dialed 911?"**

    _____

    _____

    _____

9.  **"Overlooked Heroes"**

    _____

    _____

    _____

10. **Explain why you think more pet owners keep cats than dogs. Then, tell if you would prefer a cat or dog and why.** *(Use a separate piece of paper. Each part of your answer should be one paragraph long.)*

# Missing for 28 Years

Guam, a U.S. territory, is a tropical island in the Pacific. Guam was taken over by the Japanese during World War II, but American forces reclaimed it in 1945 towards the end of the war. Instead of surrendering to the U.S. Army, some Japanese soldiers ran into the surrounding jungle and hid. One of these soldiers was a man named Shoichi Yokoi.

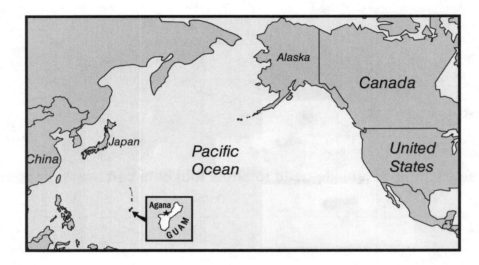

Yokoi survived for 28 years in the jungle. During all those long years, Yokoi's family was unaware that he was still alive. It wasn't until January 24, 1972, that Yokoi was discovered by two hunters who took him into custody. The hunters and everyone else who saw Yokoi were impressed by his clothes, as the fabric was made from beaten and woven plant fibers.

Once released and back in Japan, Yokoi told reporters that obtaining food was "a continuous hardship." He survived by eating mangoes, coconuts, and other jungle fruits, snails, eels, prawns, birds, and rats. He fashioned traps that he baited with grated coconut. Yokoi said that although he liked rat meat, especially the liver, he could not be concerned with taste. In order to survive, he had to eat everything he could catch.

Yokoi's shelter was a cave that he had dug completely by hand with a tiny trowel fashioned from an old cannon shell. While digging, Yokoi scattered the excavated soil, handful by handful, in a grassy area so that no one would notice it. The entrance to the cave was small and well camouflaged. It tunneled down about nine feet (3 m) before opening out (Yokoi used a bamboo ladder to get to the bottom). Yokoi could only squat in the cave, as the ceiling was low, and it was pitch-black, but Yokoi had devised a lantern that burned oil from a coconut shell.

# Jungle Friend

"Mom, is this shovel being thrown away?"

"Yes, dear," Lily's mother responded. "It's being discarded because its handle is cracked."

"Can Sergeant Fujikawa have it then?" Lily asked.

At this simple question, Lily's siblings Matt and Eliza burst out laughing. "Here we go again," they snorted gleefully. "Lily's going to tell us that her imaginary jungle friend is going to fashion it into some type of life-saving tool. Maybe he'll be digging a swimming pool now that his cave is finished."

As Lily's mother admonished her two eldest children to stop teasing their youngest sibling, she had to work at not showing her own amusement. Lily had been adamant for years that her imaginary friend was real, and she was always coming home with stories about how creative and ingenious her friend was at finding nourishment. Lily had first mentioned her imaginary friend, whom she referred to as Sergeant Fujikawa, soon after the family had moved to Guam because of Lily's father's job in the armed services.

Over the years, even as the teasing by Matt and Eliza became more merciless, Lily not only stuck with her story, but she elaborated on it. She would tell of visiting Sergeant Fujikawa's cave and how he continued to dig it out handful by handful. "He can't stand up in it," Lily would explain, "but he can stretch out when he lies down, and there's a ventilation hole in it so he doesn't have to worry about suffocating."

At first Lily's parents were really worried about her stories. Lily's father would say gently, "You know darling, the war ended nearly 20 years ago." Lily's parents had even spoken to their family doctor about Lily's stories, but she had reassured them that for many children, imaginary friends are a normal part of childhood.

# Show What You Know

*The following are questions based on the passages "Missing for 28 Years" and "Jungle Friend." If needed, you may look back at the passages to answer the questions.*

1. **Most likely Yokoi**

   (A) camouflaged the ladder with coconut.

   (B) was impressed by the ladder he used.

   (C) fashioned the tunnel ladder himself.

   (D) wove the ladder with beaten plant fibers.

2. **When Lily's mother admonished Lily's siblings, she**

   (A) amused them.

   (B) teased them.

   (C) scolded them.

   (D) discarded them.

3. **Both stories are about**

   (A) people who surrendered.

   (B) people who survived in the jungle.

   (C) people who lived in imaginary caves.

   (D) people who especially liked rat livers.

4. **One ingenious thing Yokoi did was**

   (A) make clothes from plant fibers.

   (B) remain in custody for 28 years.

   (C) eat mangoes and other jungle fruits.

   (D) not let his family know he was alive.

5. **If Lily had brought food to Yokoi, most likely Yokoi**

   (A) would have discarded it.

   (B) would not have eaten it near his cave.

   (C) would have eaten it with grated coconut.

   (D) would not have been concerned with the taste.

# Show What You Know *(cont.)*

6. **Fill in the blanks.**

   *Today's date:* _____

   *What date you might reappear if you were away as long as Yokoi:* _____

   _____

7. **Jot down a few words that describe how each character from "Jungle Friend" feels about Sergeant Fujikawa and a word or phrase from the story that supports your answer.**

   *Lily:* _____

   _____

   *Lily's parents:* _____

   _____

   *Lily's siblings:* _____

   _____

   *Lily's doctor:* _____

   _____

**Write three or four sentences that tell what each story is about.**

8. **"Missing for 28 Years"**

   _____

   _____

   _____

9. **"Jungle Friend"**

   _____

   _____

   _____

10. **Decide if you think Lily's friend is imaginary or not. Write one or two paragraphs where you defend your answer. Use information from both stories in your answer.** *(Use a separate piece of paper. Your writing should be a few paragraphs long.)*

# State Quarters

Since 1999, the U.S. Mint has issued five quarters a year, with a 10-week interval between each coin. Each quarter commemorates one of the 50 United States. The quarters are issued in the order that the states joined the Union. Delaware was first, and Hawaii was last.

The quarters are only issued once, but the number of quarters minted each year is not the same. The number minted is not determined by a state's population. It is not determined by the popularity of the quarter design. The number minted is reflective of the national economy's need for quarters at the time the coin is issued. For example, 1.5 billion Virginia quarters were minted in 2000, whereas a mere 448.8 million Maine quarters were minted in 2003.

One of the design rules was that "no portrait of a living person may be included in the design of any quarter dollar." Some wonder if Ohio's quarter design is breaking a federal law. Ohio's quarter depicts an astronaut superimposed on the outline of the state and standing alongside the Wright brothers' famed flyer. The phrase "Birthplace of Aviation Pioneers" is also on the coin. One would think that the astronaut would be John Glenn or Neil Armstrong. Glenn and Armstrong were both space pioneers. Glenn was the first American to be put into orbital spaceflight, and Armstrong was the first man to walk on the moon. Both men were born in Ohio, and they both attended—while alive, of course—the official launch of the state quarter.

Design rules also stated that suitable subject matter included "state landmarks (natural and man-made), landscapes..." New Hampshire's quarter depicts a distinctive granite rock formation known as the "Old Man of the Mountain." Less than three years after the quarter was issued, the age-old rock formation collapsed!

# State Quarter Trivia Quiz

"It's Trivia Quiz Day," Mr. Holt told his history class, "with today's subject being state quarters. The definition of trivia is 'small, unimportant matters.' Although trivial facts may seem trifling and unimportant, they can be interesting and help us learn. Who knows which state quarter depicts a diamond?"

Kamala answered, "Arkansas's quarter depicts a diamond. Arkansas has the only state park where visitors can prospect for diamonds and keep what they find. Since the park was opened in 1972, prospectors have found over 25,000 diamonds. One of the diamonds sold for $34,000 dollars!"

"Your answer is a real gem," Mr. Holt told Kamala. "Not only is it correct, but it's filled with interesting trivia. Now, who knows which state quarter depicts a fruit that isn't native to the state?"

Roberto answered, "The fruit is a peach, and the state is Georgia. Peaches can be dated back to 5th century B.C.E. China, but their start in Georgia began approximately in 1571. This was when Franciscan monks introduced the fruit, along with artichokes, citrus, figs, olives, and onions, at Spain's coastal missions running through the coastal islands."

"A real peach of an answer," Mr. Holt told Roberto. "Now, who knows which state quarter has raised Braille dots?"

"Alabama!" cried out Sabrina. "Alabama's quarter depicts Helen Keller, a woman who, despite being both blind and deaf, learned to communicate by reading signs spelled into her hand, as well as by Braille. When Keller graduated from Radcliffe College in 1904, she was the first deaf-blind person to ever earn a university degree."

"More than just Keller's head or bust is depicted because the rules say that 'no head and shoulders portrait or bust of any person, living or dead' can be part of the design," Kevin added.

"A complete and well-communicated answer!" laughed Mr. Holt.

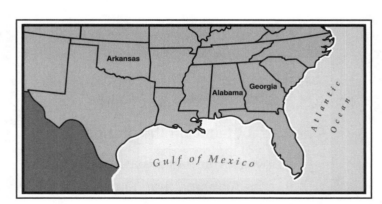

# Show What You Know

*The following are questions based on the passages "State Quarters" and "State Quarter Trivia Quiz." If needed, you may look back at the passages to answer the questions.*

1. **The number of quarters minted is reflective**

   (A) of the national economy.

   (B) of the state's population.

   (C) of the popularity of the design.

   (D) of the order in which the state joined the Union.

2. **What food was not introduced by monks?**

   (A) figs

   (B) onions

   (C) olives

   (D) squash

3. **What do both stories have in common?**

   (A) information about fruit on state quarters

   (B) information about landmarks on state quarters

   (C) information about rules for state-quarter designs

   (D) information about the minting order for state quarters

4. **What could not be part of a state quarter design?**

   (A) a printed word

   (B) a racecar and a racetrack

   (C) a bust of an early president

   (D) a landscape with a living tree

5. **One cannot tell from the stories**

   (A) if any quarter has a state outline on it.

   (B) if more Alabama than Maine quarters were minted.

   (C) if Helen Keller was able to earn her university degree.

   (D) if one could prospect for diamonds after 1972 in Arkansas.

70

# Show What You Know *(cont.)*

6. **Write down five facts about the U.S. Mint state quarter program.**

   a. _____

   b. _____

   c. _____

   d. _____

   e. _____

7. **Keep it straight! Fill in the chart with the names of each student, what question they answered, and the correct state answer.**

| Name | Question | State |
|------|----------|-------|
|      |          |       |
|      |          |       |
|      |          |       |

**Write three or four sentences that tell what each story is about.**

8. **"State Quarters"**

   _____

   _____

   _____

9. **"State Quarter Trivia Quiz"**

   _____

   _____

   _____

10. **Decide if you think Ohio broke the rules with its quarter design. Describe the design, which rule it might have broken, and your reasoning behind your answer. Remember that if you state the rule exactly as written, it must be in quotation marks.** *(Use a separate piece of paper. Your writing should be a few paragraphs long.)*

# Jumping from the Stratosphere

The stratosphere is a region of the Earth's atmosphere above the troposphere. It begins at an altitude of 7–10 miles (11.3 to 16.1 km) and extends to about 30 miles (48.3 km) above the Earth. The stratosphere is not a hospitable place for life. Joseph Kittinger, Jr., while a captain in the Air Force, jumped from the stratosphere three times.

Kittinger made his final jump on August 16, 1960. He was in a helium balloon with an open gondola 102,800 feet (31,300 m) above the Earth. At this elevation, the atmosphere is so thin that one's body fluids begin to boil. The fluids do not boil because of the heat; they boil because the atmosphere is so thin that there is not enough air pressure to keep water a liquid so it turns to gas. Kittinger ascended into the air in a balloon and set the world's record for highest balloon ascent. When he jumped, he set the world's record for the highest parachute jump.

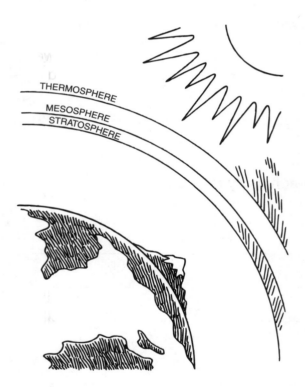

Kittinger fell for 4 minutes and 36 seconds before he opened his chute. During his fall, Kittinger almost broke the sound barrier. He reached a maximum speed of 614 mph (988 km/h or 274 m/s), setting the world's record for fastest speed by a human through the atmosphere. Kittinger wore a pressurized suit with a sealed helmet for his jump. In addition to being pressurized, the suit was electrically heated. This was necessary because at one point the temperature gauge on Kittinger's suit registered close to 100 degrees below zero.

Kittinger was unharmed by his descent, except for his right hand. Due to a malfunction of Kittinger's pressure suit, the glove had failed to pressurize, causing Kittinger's hand to inflate and swell to twice its normal size. Fortunately for Kittinger, the swelling eventually went down.

# Jolon's Hero

Jolon took a deep breath to quell his nervousness and then began his oral report: "We were told to report on a person we personally think is a hero," Jolon said, "and I chose an Air Force captain named Joseph Kittinger, Jr., who jumped three times from the stratosphere. Records from his third and final jump in 1960 will probably never be matched."

"So he's your hero because of the world records?" Devon interrupted.

"No," Jolon explained, "he's my hero because he jumped again after his first jump on November 16, 1959. For Kittinger's first jump, he rode a balloon to 76,400 feet (23,287 m), a height nearly twice as high as anyone had fallen before. When he went to unhook himself from the gondola, he found that he couldn't move because the equipment kit that hung from the bottom of his suit had become wedged into the seat as the pressure dropped. His delay jumping meant that his first parachute, which was timed to open automatically, was released 14 seconds too early, when he was falling too slowly for it to fill with air.

"Rather than stabilize his fall, the chute wrapped around Kittinger's neck. Kittinger was unconscious when his second chute opened, failed to fill with air, and coiled around his body. Kittinger began a flat spin, reaching 80 revolutions per minute, before a third, automatic reserve chute opened and saved his life."

"Unbelievable!" Paige said. "I can't believe he survived."

"What's truly unbelievable," Jolon went on, "is that despite his near fatal experience, Kittinger was willing to jump again! Before making his final jump, Kittinger told his crew over the radio, 'Man will never conquer space. He will learn to live with it, but he will never conquer it.'"

# Show What You Know

*The following are questions based on the passages "Jumping from the Stratosphere" and "Jolon's Hero." If needed, you may look back at the passages to answer the questions.*

1. **Body fluids begin to boil in the stratosphere because**

   (A) of the low air pressure.

   (B) of the high temperature.

   (C) of gases turning to liquids.

   (D) of the pressure from the troposphere.

2. **Before Kittinger's first jump, approximately what was the record for the highest parachute jump?**

   (A) 14,500 feet (4,420 m)

   (B) 25,100 feet (7,650 m)

   (C) 38,200 feet (11,644 m)

   (D) 47,300 feet (14,417 m)

3. **What do both stories have in common?**

   (A) They are both about Jolon's final jump.

   (B) They are both about Jolon's oral report.

   (C) They are both about Jolon's world records.

   (D) They are both about Jolon's hero Joseph Kittinger, Jr.

4. **One can tell that Kittinger was in the balloon gondola by himself because he alone set the record for**

   (A) the highest balloon ascent.

   (B) the highest parachute jump.

   (C) the longest time in a pressurized suit.

   (D) the fastest speed by a human through the atmosphere.

5. **From the stories, what can one tell about Kittinger's second jump?**

   (A) It took place in 1960.

   (B) The reserve chute automatically opened.

   (C) Kittinger was unconscious during part of his fall.

   (D) It didn't make Kittinger feel closer to conquering space.

74

# Show What You Know (cont.)

6. **Fill in the blanks with information about Kittinger using facts from the story "Jumping from the Stratosphere."**

   a. Who was he? _a cpt in us_

   b. From where did he jump? _atmousphere_

   c. How high did he ascend? _102,800_

   d. When did he jump? _102,800_

   e. Why did he wear a pressurized suit? _top protect for cold und heat_

   f. What records did he set? _highst jump_

7. **Fill in the chart with information about what happened with Kittinger's three chutes on his first jump.**

| Chute One | Chute Two | Chute Three |
|---|---|---|
| failed choked him | worked | Worked |

**Write three or four sentences that tell what each story is about.**

8. **"Jumping from the Stratosphere"**
   _a dude who has the world reckord for jumping._

9. **"Jolon's Hero"**
   _A person who wrote a story about kittinger._

10. **Think of someone you consider a hero. Write one or two paragraphs where you provide information that answers the *what, when, how, who, why,* and *where* questions about the person. Explain why this person is a hero to you. The person you choose to write about may be a public or private person.** *(Use a separate piece of paper.)*

# How a Flavor Reached the United States

Thomas Jefferson is known for many things. He was a founding father. He was principal author of the Declaration of Independence. He was president from 1801 to 1809. He arranged for the Louisiana Purchase. He founded the University of Virginia. All of these accomplishments are well known, but Jefferson did something else, too: he introduced a flavor to the newly formed United States.

***Thomas Jefferson***

Vanilla is derived from an orchid. There are over 35,000 different species of orchid, but vanilla is the only flavor ever derived from them. Vanilla is native to the tropical regions of Central America. It is also native to the northernmost regions of South America. Long ago the Totonac people of Mexico learned to cultivate the vanilla plant. They learned to process its seed pod, drying and grinding it so it would release its hidden flavor. The Totonacs used vanilla whenever they prepared a drink we know today as chocolate.

***vanilla orchid plant***

The Aztecs were also a people of long-ago Mexico. They conquered the Totonacs around 1425. Part of the tribute the Aztecs insisted the Totonacs pay was vanilla. Hernan Cortes was a Spanish conqueror. He first tasted chocolate and its added vanilla when it was offered to him by the Aztecs in 1519. When Cortes returned to Europe, he brought back vanilla seed pods to be used in the preparation of chocolate.

Europeans didn't realize vanilla was a delicious flavor in its own right until 1602. The discovery was made by Hugh Morgan. Morgan's job was to prepare herbal medicines for Queen Elizabeth I. Queen Elizabeth adored the taste, and its popularity spread. Jefferson first tasted vanilla when he was the minister to France in 1785. When Jefferson returned home, he carried vanilla pods with him so that he could introduce the flavor to his young country.

# All Things Vanilla

"Do you want more dessert?" Victoria's Aunt Ruthie asked her.

"Thank you, but I've really had enough," said Victoria, just managing to mask a groan. Victoria was visiting her Aunt Ruthie and Uncle Domingo for a week, and though Victoria had enjoyed the food at first, she had grown tired of it. For some reason, every bit of food her aunt and uncle prepared was flavored with copious amounts of vanilla. At first Victoria could well understand how someone could adore the taste of vanilla. After all, her aunt and uncle were amazing cooks, and the pastries, cookies, and other treats they churned out were delectable. But by the third day, Victoria was wondering if there was anything her aunt and uncle ate that didn't taste of vanilla.

"Aunt Ruthie," Victoria asked, "have you ever thought about cooking something flavored with chocolate, strawberry, butterscotch, lemon, or even mint?"

"Oh, I couldn't do that," her aunt had replied. "Even though I'm tired of vanilla, I wouldn't want to disappoint your uncle. The very first time I cooked for him, I thought I'd ruined the entire meal. I accidentally spilled a bottle of vanilla on everything; but your uncle ate every bite! Since then, I've put copious amounts of vanilla in everything just to please him."

At the end of her visit, Victoria's uncle treated her to a trip to a restaurant. Much to Victoria's surprise, her uncle ordered a chocolate brownie and a strawberry shake. "I thought you loved vanilla," said Victoria in surprise.

"Whatever gave you that idea?" her uncle said, astonished. "I can't stand it, but I know your aunt loves it because from the very first meal she prepared, she's always added large amounts of vanilla. I don't complain because I want her to eat what she likes."

# Show What You Know

*The following are based on "How a Flavor Reached the United States" and "All Things Vanilla." If needed, you may look back at the passages to answer the questions.*

1. **Which statement is false?**

   Ⓐ Queen Elizabeth I adored the taste of vanilla.

   Ⓑ Vanilla was used to enhance the flavor of chocolate.

   Ⓒ People in Mexico first learned to cultivate vanilla.

   Ⓓ Jefferson brought back vanilla after he was president.

2. **If something is copious,**

   Ⓐ it is tasteful.

   Ⓑ it is flavorful.

   Ⓒ it is plentiful.

   Ⓓ it is wonderful.

3. **What do both stories have in common?**

   Ⓐ a flavor native to Europe

   Ⓑ a favorite flavor of Cortes

   Ⓒ a flavor derived from an orchid

   Ⓓ a flavor used only with chocolate

4. **What statement can one be most certain about?**

   Ⓐ Queen Elizabeth adored vanilla more than Victoria did.

   Ⓑ Queen Elizabeth adored vanilla more than Jefferson did.

   Ⓒ Queen Elizabeth adored vanilla more than Aunt Ruthie did.

   Ⓓ Queen Elizabeth adored vanilla more than Uncle Domingo did.

5. **From the stories, one can tell that Victoria's aunt and uncle**

   Ⓐ want to please each other.

   Ⓑ want restaurants to use more vanilla.

   Ⓒ want more people to cultivate vanilla.

   Ⓓ want more flavors native to tropical regions.

# Show What You Know *(cont.)*

6. **Use information from the story "How a Flavor Reached the United States" to fill in the timeline. Use every date mentioned in the story.**

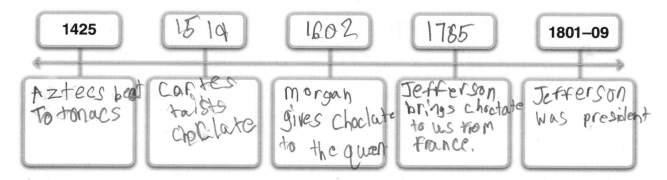

| 1425 | 1519 | 1602 | 1785 | 1801–09 |
| --- | --- | --- | --- | --- |
| Aztecs beat Totonacs | Cartes taists chocolate | morgan gives choclate to the queen | Jefferson brings choclate to us from France. | Jefferson was president |

7. **Write down the name of the characters from "All Things Vanilla" and in what paragraph you first found out how they really felt about vanilla.**

| Paragraph # | Character | Feelings About Vanilla |
| --- | --- | --- |
| 4 | Aunt ruthie | old |
| 1 | victoria | old |
| 6 | uncle domingo | old |

**Write three or four sentences that tell what each story is about.**

8. **"How a Flavor Reached the United States"**

First vinilla started in Central Amarica. Then it was taken to Eroupe. Later Jefferson took it to the U.S.

9. **"All Things Vanilla"**

Victora is staying at here ant and uncle's. she is bord of vanilla. Her ant thinks her uncle likes it. Her uncle desent want to be rude and say he is bord of the flavor.

10. **Think about what Victoria found out about her aunt and uncle's feelings about vanilla. Do you think she should tell her aunt and uncle what she found out? Explain what you think Victoria should do and why.** *(Use a separate piece of paper. Your writing should be one paragraph long.)*

# A Conundrum on the Nazca Plain

Straight lines on the Nazca Plain in Peru presented a conundrum. Scientists believed the lines were made long ago, somewhere between 200 B.C.E. and 600 C.E. They knew that the lines were made by scraping away the top layer of rocky soil so that the different-colored ground beneath was revealed. They knew that the some of the lines formed parallel tracks, while others intersected.

The conundrum presented itself when the scientists looked at the lines from an aerial view. Some of the lines formed enormous animals and birds. For example, one bird, a condor, was 445 foot (135 m) long. Aircraft was invented 1,500 years after the Nazca people made the pictures, so how were the pictures formed, and why were they made?

Many people believed that the lines formed a landing strip made by extraterrestrials, or aliens, from outer space. These people said the Nazca people didn't have the intelligence or materials to accomplish such a feat on their own. A man named Jack Nickell rebutted this theory by reproducing an exact copy of the giant condor in Kentucky. Nickell used only sticks and string, as these materials were available to the Nazca people. He used a grid system where each square from a tiny drawing was made many times bigger on the ground.

The how of the conundrum was answered by Nickell, but not the why. By accident, scientist Paul Kosok discovered that on the shortest day of the year, one of the main lines pointed directly at the horizon where the sun set. Investigating further, he found that other lines matched other points on the calendar. By using computer programs, scientists have discovered that the lines form a star map. The star map matches the night sky between 200 B.C.E. and 600 C.E.

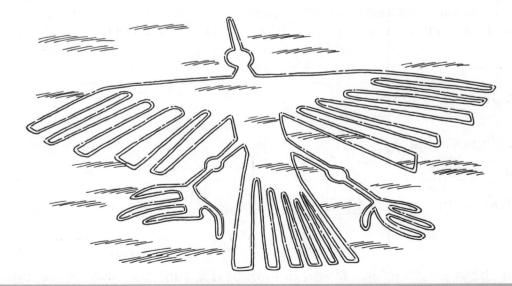

# A Rules Conundrum

Mr. Pythagorean, a city bus driver, told his children Lawrence and Michelle that evening at dinner, "I had a passenger with a conundrum today."

Michelle said, "Is a conundrum some type of large package or something?"

Lawrence answered his little sister's question by explaining, "A conundrum is an exceedingly difficult problem or question where the answer may only be a guess."

Upon hearing the definition of a conundrum, Michelle turned to her father and said, "You have piqued my curiosity. What was your passenger's conundrum?"

Mr. Pythagorean explained, "The passenger was a boy who had just bought a fishing rod that was five feet (1.5 m) long. The boy had no other way to get home except by bus, but there's a city ordinance that prohibits anyone carrying packages on the bus longer than four feet (1.2 m)."

"Are you saying that you didn't allow him to board?" demanded Michelle.

"I couldn't let him disobey the rules," Mr. Pythagorean said, "but I found a solution to his conundrum."

"The conundrum being how to get on a bus without breaking the ordinance about the package length with an object longer than what the ordinance allows," said Michelle. "Dad, that's impossible unless he bent the rod, took it apart, or altered it in some other fashion!"

"No, it's not," said Lawrence, grinning. "I know what you had the boy do so he could board the bus with his oversize package and not break the city ordinance."

"What?" demanded Michelle.

"You had the boy get a box that was three feet by four feet (.9 by 1.2 m). Then you had the boy place the rod in the box because the diagonal of a three-by-four box is equal to five."

"Exactly!" Mr. Pythagorean said with a smile.

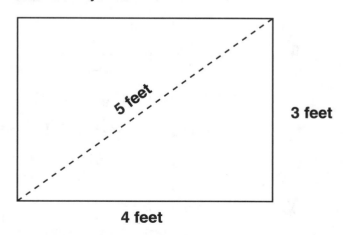

5 feet

3 feet

4 feet

# Show What You Know

*The following are based on "A Conundrum on the Nazca Plain" and "A Rules Conundrum."*
*If needed, you may look back at the passages to answer the questions.*

1. **One can tell from the story "A Conundrum on the Nazca Plain" that**

   (A) the night sky has changed over time.

   (B) the Nazca people had invented aircraft.

   (C) scientists accomplish everything by accident.

   (D) the pictures couldn't have been formed with the materials at hand.

2. **What question could be called a conundrum?**

   (A) What came first:  milk or soda pop?

   (B) What came first:  the car or the plane?

   (C) What came first:  fire or the microwave?

   (D) What came first:  the chicken or the egg?

3. **What did you read about in both stories?**

   (A) conundrums

   (B) unsolved conundrums

   (C) easily solved conundrums

   (D) one unsolved and one solved conundrum

4. **Using a grid system where a square from a tiny drawing is made bigger, a three-by-four box with a diagonal of five might be redrawn as a**

   (A) 6 by 8 box with a diagonal of 15

   (B) 9 by 12 box with a diagonal of 15

   (C) 8 by 16 box with a diagonal of 15

   (D) 12 by 19 box with a diagonal of 15

5. **The Nazca people may have had**

   (A) some type of bus.

   (B) some type of aircraft.

   (C) some type of ordinances.

   (D) some type of computer programs.

# Show What You Know (cont.)

6. **Draw a set of parallel lines and a set of intersecting lines. Label each set.**

   Drawing: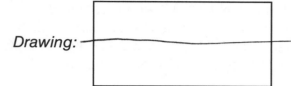

   Drawing:

   Label: _____

   Label: _____

7. **Draw a three-by-four box (use centimeters). Measure the diagonal.**

**Write three or four sentences that tell what each story is about.**

8. **"A Conundrum on the Nazca Plain"**

   This is about the Plain in Nazca
   The people Made huge pictures in the ground
   They were a resemblence the the stars.

9. **"A Rules Conundrum"**

   This is about a busdriver
   They find a kid that can't get on the bus
   he fixes the problem.

10. **On a separate piece of paper, describe a conundrum and a possible solution. Your conundrum can be a made-up puzzle or something out of real life. If you do not want to think up your own conundrum, describe one of the two below, adding details to the story outline and a solution:**

    ✤ *There is an accident involving a father and son. A surgeon rushes in. Surgeon says,"This boy is my son. I can't operate on him."*

    ✤ *It is a clear night, and many stars are visible. A son asks his father to point out the North Star. The father says,"That's not possible."*

# A Lifetime of Names

A famous Native American doctor was given three names over his lifetime. The doctor's first name was "Wassaja," which in the doctor's native tribal language of Yavapai means "Beckoning." Wassaja was kidnapped in October 1871 by the Pima. The Pima were longtime enemies of the Yavapai.

Wassaja was only five years old when he was kidnapped from his village in Arizona. On this night of terror, he was separated from his family, bound with rope, and forced to watch his village burn. When Wassaja was taken to his captor's village, it was on a horse—a creature he had never seen before.

**Dr. Carlos Montezuma**

The Pima renamed Wassaja, calling him "Hejelweiikan," which means "left alone." In November 1871, the Pima took Wassaja to be sold as a slave. On the way, they stopped at a house, where Wassaja was led into a dark stockroom. There, Wassaja saw a boy about the same size as himself and whose eyes wouldn't leave Wassaja's. The boy copied everything Wassaja did, but when Wassaja jumped up, the boy disappeared. It wasn't until many years later that Wassaja realized he had been looking in a mirror at his own image.

A man named Carlo Gentile bought Wassaja. Gentile was a photographer from Italy. Gentile didn't want a slave, but he felt sorry for the little boy he saw being sold. When Gentile adopted Wassaja, he renamed him "Carlos Montezuma"—the "Carlos" after himself, and the "Montezuma" for some ruins near Wassaja's native home. Wassaja became a doctor and an activist for Native American rights. Wassaja died in January 1923, but he is remembered for his words: "'What can I get?' is a fatal question for a man. . . The true query of a man, even one who would get much is, 'What can I give?'"

# Why the Doctor Didn't Vote

On the first Tuesday in November, Ms. McCarthy said, "Class, today is election day. It is the day United States citizens can vote for their president. They can vote for other members of their government, too. You've just finished the biography of Dr. Carlos Montezuma. Tell me why the good doctor never voted."

"He couldn't," Marcus answered. "He wasn't a United States citizen."

"Right," said Venice. "Dr. Montezuma advocated for the rights of Native Americans. He was appalled at the wretched living conditions on reservations. He believed that Native Americans needed opportunities to grow and that those opportunities could only happen through education and by receiving U.S. citizenship."

"Dr. Montezuma died in 1923. The Indian Citizenship Act wasn't passed until June 2, 1924," Courtney said.

"What exactly did the Indian Citizenship Act say?" queried Loretta.

"It declared all non-citizen Indians born within the United States to be citizens, giving them the right to vote," Patrick answered.

"Do you think Dr. Montezuma would vote if he were alive today?" asked Ms. McCarthy.

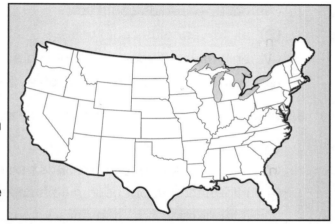

"Definitely," answered Patrick. "The doctor worked for the right of citizenship. With that right comes the privilege of voting. Dr. Montezuma would not have wasted his opportunity to have a say in the government."

"Right," said Venice, "because on election day, all male and female citizens over the age of 18 can cast a vote."

"Females could vote starting in 1920, when the 19th Amendment was finally ratified," Loretta said.

"It was in 1971 that the 26th Amendment gave 18-year-olds the right to vote," Courtney said.

"I think what would surprise Dr. Montezuma today," Marcus said, "is how many people don't bother to exercise their right to vote. Perhaps they don't understand how hard people had to work to earn that privilege."

# Show What You Know

*The following are questions based on the passages "A Lifetime of Names" and "Why the Doctor Didn't Vote." If needed, you may look back at the passages to answer the questions.*

1. **About how long after Wassaja was kidnapped was he sold as a slave?**

   (A) about 1 month
   (B) about 3 months
   (C) about 5 months
   (D) about 13 months

2. **When Dr. Montezuma died,**

   (A) no 18-year-olds could vote.
   (B) all 18-year-olds could vote.
   (C) only male 18-year-olds could vote.
   (D) some 18-year-old citizens could vote.

3. **What do both stories have in common?**

   (A) information about voting
   (B) information about the doctor's name
   (C) information about becoming a citizen
   (D) information about someone who believed in giving

4. **From the stories, one can tell that Carlo Gentile**

   (A) didn't think Wassaja should be a citizen.
   (B) provided Wassaja with an opportunity to grow.
   (C) wanted Wassaja to exercise the right to vote.
   (D) was interested in what he could get out of Wassaja.

5. **Most likely, Wassaja thought there**

   (A) was not a good reason to become a citizen.
   (B) should not be an amendment allowing women to vote.
   (C) ought to be more people asking for what they can get.
   (D) were too few educational opportunities on reservations.

86

# Show What You Know (cont.)

6. **Fill in each top box in order of how they were given with one of the doctor's names. In each bottom box, jot down some information about the name.**

| Beginning | Middle | End |
|---|---|---|
| he was born | he was stolen | he was bought |

7. **Many different speakers were in the story "Why the Doctor Didn't Vote." Keep them straight by writing down their names in the order that they spoke.**

1. Venice
2. Marces
3. Courtnee
4. Loretta
5. patric
6. 
7. Ms. McCarthy
8. 
9. 
10. 
11. 
12. 

**Write three or four sentences that tell what each story is about.**

8. **"A Lifetime of Names"**

a boy is stolen bought and given freedom

9. **"Why the Doctor Didn't Vote"**

The history of amarican voting sistem.

10. **Decide how Dr. Montezuma might feel about people who do not exercise their right to vote today. Then, write dialogue (the speaker may be you, Dr. Montezuma, or someone else) in which Dr. Montezuma's position is explained. Include some true biographical facts about Dr. Montezuma in your dialogue.** *(Use a separate piece of paper. Your writing should be a few paragraphs long.)*

# Masters of Understatement

Greg Child, a climber and writer, discusses in one essay the differences between the "total disclosure" practices of today and the "less is more" tradition. He gives two powerful examples of climbers who upheld the "less is more" tradition and were masters of the understatement.

**Sir Edmund Hillary**

Sir Edmund Hillary is known for being the first to successfully climb Mt. Everest, the world's highest mountain. Hillary was also part of an expedition to Antarctica and the South Pole. Traveling in a convoy of tractors, expedition members were in constant danger due to huge crevasses that could easily swallow a house.

When Child heard Hillary speak, Hillary illustrated this point by describing a tractor driven by Jim Bates. Without warning, the tractor broke through a snow bridge, slipping backward into a crevasse. The only thing keeping Bates from death was that the tractor's cabin had jammed in the mouth of the slot. Hillary described how he walked to the edge of the crevasse, peered in, and saw Jim's face through the cabin window. "Hello, Jim, how are you down there?" he said. "I'm okay," Jim replied, "but I don't like the view."

Child's second example was taken from an article by Doug Scott in which he described an epic in the Karakorum Mountain range of India and Pakistan. Scott's climbing partner Chris Bonington had rappelled down from a 24,000-foot (7,315 m) summit, only to find that Scott had injured his legs. Rather than go into details and vivid descriptions of the near-death experience and excruciating pain he suffered, Scott simply disclosed the dialogue that followed:

"'What, ho!' Chris said cheerily."

"'I've broken my right leg and smashed the left ankle,' I said."

"'We'll just work on getting you down,' he replied airily. 'Don't worry. You're a long way from death.'"

# How It Went

Gabriella and Sarah's progress up the treacherous slopes of K2 was a race with a bank of black clouds. Gabriella and Sarah had planned and trained for the assault on K2, a peak in the Karakorum Range and the second-highest mountain in the world, with great care, but now they were exhausted, oxygen-depleted, and suffering from excruciating hunger.

Although they were at the limit of their physical and mental endurance, they still desired to press on. They knew they were close to the summit, as they were now looking down on surrounding peaks that once towered over them. Numerous climbers had perished on K2, their bodies lost forever on the treacherous slopes, but Gabriella and Sarah believed that they could succeed.

Suddenly, the storm let loose. Instantly, Gabriella and Sarah were blinded, unable to see even their gloved hands in front of their faces. Sharp particles of snow cut their already-frozen faces, and their already-numbed toes and fingers began to freeze. Sarah knew that there was no option but to turn back. She led the way, finding every foothold with her axe alone, for there was no sign of the steps they had painfully cut into the ice on the way up.

It took 17 hours for the two climbers to reach their highest camp. There, they had to huddle for four days in a tiny, cramped tent, only leaving it to shovel away the snow that threatened to bury and suffocate them. It took them two more days to descend, their route no longer recognizable due to recent avalanches, and reach the safety of their base camp. Once there, Sarah was asked by another climber, "How'd it go?"

Sarah replied, "I'd say it went well."

"How can you say that?" Gabriella gasped.

"We're alive," Sarah said

# Show What You Know

*The following are questions based on the passages "Masters of Understatement" and "How It Went." If needed, you may look back at the passages to answer the questions.*

1. **After reading "Masters of Understatement," one does not know if in Child's essay there was**

    Ⓐ an example with climbers.

    Ⓑ an example of "total disclosure."

    Ⓒ an example of the "less is more" tradition.

    Ⓓ an example with the first man to summit Everest.

2. **How many days did it take Gabriella and Sarah to descend from their highest camp to their base camp?**

    Ⓐ two

    Ⓑ four

    Ⓒ nine

    Ⓓ seventeen

3. **What do both stories have in common?**

    Ⓐ dialogues about successful climbs

    Ⓑ dialogues filled with vivid descriptions

    Ⓒ dialogues that understate the danger faced

    Ⓓ dialogues between writers and expedition members

4. **When something is excruciating it is**

    Ⓐ cold and dangerous.

    Ⓑ agonizing and extreme.

    Ⓒ powerful and recognizable

    Ⓓ treacherous and suffocating.

5. **Greg Child would most likely consider Sarah to be a climber who followed the "less is more" tradition because**

    Ⓐ she came close to experiencing death.

    Ⓑ she had to turn back before summiting K2.

    Ⓒ she disclosed the dialogue between she and Gabriella.

    Ⓓ she did not go into details about the danger she faced.

# Show What You Know (cont.)

6. **Fill in the details using the two examples described by Greg Child.**

|  | Example 1 | Example 2 |
|---|---|---|
| Who | Sir Edmund hillary | Dug Scott |
| Where | South Pole | Karakoum Mountian rang |
| What | ex Ploring | rappelling |

7. **In the box to the right, draw a rough sketch of K2, marking the following according to "How It Went":**

    **A** base camp

    **B** the summit

    **C** highest camp

    **D** a recent avalanche area

    **E** where Sarah and Gabriella might have reached

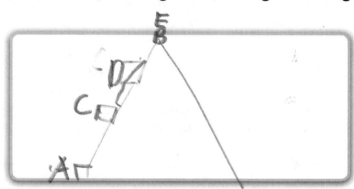

**Write three or four sentences that tell what each story is about.**

8. **"Masters of Understatement"**

People concering changes
They were Climbing mountions
there were exploring the antart's

9. **"How It Went"**

People atempting to climb K2
They turnded back.
They retreaded safely

10. **On a separate piece of paper, write one paragraph in the "total disclosure" practice where you describe in excruciating detail an event or something that happened to you or someone else. Then in a second paragraph, use the "less is more" tradition to relate the same event.** *(Note that the second paragraph may end up being very short!)*

# The Misnamed Predator

Killer whales are misnamed. Although they are powerful predators, they aren't whales. Killer whales belong to the scientific family *Delphinidae*, which includes dolphins and porpoises. The origins of the misleading name began back in the 18th century. This was when whalers nicknamed these animals "whale killers" after witnessing their fierce and powerful attacks on much larger prey. Over time, the name became reversed, and the animals became known as "killer whales."

Despite the popularity of the name "killer whale," scientists aren't comfortable with it because of its inaccuracy. They prefer the name "orca." "Orca" comes from the creature's scientific name, *Orcinus orca*. As the name "orca" avoids the word "whale," it is a much better fit for the largest member of the dolphin family. In addition, the negative feelings that one gets from the word "killer" are avoided.

Orcas hunt in groups. Their particular hunting method depends on the circumstances and their prey. Around ice, an orca may spy hop (poke its head out of the water and look around). If prey is spotted on a floe, the orca signals other members of its pod, or group, and then swims underneath the edge of the floe. Next, it pushes the floe up, forcing the resting animals to slide down into the water where the other pod members are waiting.

Orcas along the beaches of Punta Norte, Argentina, and the Crozet Islands in the southern Indian Ocean use a hunting technique that involves surging out of the water and landing on shore. Orcas will rush out of the water and land so quickly that they can grab unsuspecting seals and sea lions before their victims are even aware that an attack is underway. Then, with their prey clamped firmly between their jaws, the orcas wriggle back into the sea.

# Letter from an Exchange Student

24 Calle Norte
Puerto Deseado
Argentina

January 15, 2010

Dear Mom and Dad,

Yesterday my science class went on a whale-watching field trip. We went with a professor who has been studying a population of right whales that live off the coast of Argentina since 1969. Right whales are the most endangered of all the great whales. Despite being protected since the 1930s, no one knows if the population will ever recover.

Right whales belong to the scientific family *Balaenidae*, but their common name came from whalers. The whalers called this type of whales "right whales" because they were the "right" whale to kill. They were filled with oil harvested and sold for commercial reasons, easy targets because they swam slowly, and floated when they were dead.

We saw the right whales, but we also saw orcas (you might know them as "killer whales"). The professor told us that orcas are amazing predators. They teach their young different hunting methods for the hundreds of different types of animals they eat. Among other things, orcas eat fish, squid, seabirds, otters, penguins, sea turtles, seals, sea lions, polar bears, walruses, and whales.

When one of my classmates heard that orcas working together can attack much larger whales, he suggested that perhaps the orcas were the reason the right whale population was so endangered. The professor explained that even though orcas are at the top of the ocean food chain, it was overhunting by whalers who caused the near-extinction of right whales. He also told us something that surprised me and the rest of the class. He said that 40 to 50 percent of all orca calves die within the first year of birth. I guess survival is always hard—even for a top predator.

Until next week,

Gwendolyn

# Show What You Know

*The following are based on "The Misnamed Predator" and "Letter from an Exchange Student." If needed, you may look back at the passages to answer the questions.*

1. **Scientists prefer the name "orca" because**

   Ⓐ orcas are powerful predators.

   Ⓑ orcas eat many different kinds of prey.

   Ⓒ the name "whale killer" reversed over time.

   ⬤ orcas are members of the dolphin family.

2. **Which answer is not a reason why right whales were hunted?**

   Ⓐ swam slowly

   Ⓑ filled with oil

   Ⓒ floated when dead

   ⬤ top of the food chain

3. **What do both stories have in common?**

   ⬤ animals that eat seals

   Ⓑ animals that are protected

   Ⓒ animals that hunt together

   Ⓓ animals that are near extinction

4. **From the stories, one can tell that 18th-century whalers were definitely witness to orcas**

   ⬤ hunting together.

   Ⓑ protecting their calves.

   Ⓒ spy hopping to spot prey.

   Ⓓ surging out of the water.

5. **From the stories, one can tell that right whales**

   Ⓐ eat hundreds of types of animals.

   ⬤ are not in the same family as dolphins.

   Ⓒ are above orcas on the ocean food chain.

   Ⓓ live only in the coastal waters of Argentina.

94

# Show What You Know (cont.)

6. Write down the steps an orca follows when it catches an animal resting on an ice floe.

| 1. Signls others | 2. 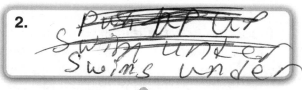 ~~Push up up~~ ~~Swim under~~ Swims under |
|---|---|

| 4. pod members wait at other end of floe | 3.  Push up |

7. Fill in the names of some animals to complete the food chain.

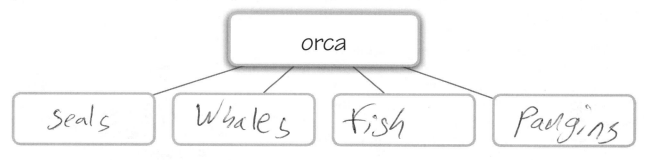

orca

| seals | Whales | fish | Pangins |

Write three or four sentences that tell what each story is about.

8. "The Misnamed Predator"

This is about the orca.
Killer whale is a Bad name.
They hunt seals whales fish and pangins.
They live in Puget Sorte, Anderdang, and Coozer Island.

9. "Letter from an Exchange Student"

A students goes whale watching
They see a might Whale
the tour guid talks about them.
The student is amazed.

10. Imagine that you were able to see orcas hunting seals on land or on an ice floe. In a letter to a friend, describe what you saw, as well as provide some information about orcas. Remember to include the parts of a letter, such as the date, a greeting, and a closing. (Use a separate piece of paper. Your letter should be one or two paragraphs long.)

# When No Whistle Blew

Jean Driscoll, born November 18, 1966, was 16 years old and in high school when she first participated in the Milwaukee Public Schools division of Recreation Wheelchair Sports Program. At first Driscoll was embarrassed to be there, but one incident changed her mind. At the very start of her first soccer game, she witnessed two players in manual wheelchairs whiz down the court from opposite ends toward a big red rubber ball. Intent on gaining possession of the ball, the two players whammed into each other so forcefully that one player was catapulted out of his chair and onto the court.

Driscoll expected a whistle to blow. She expected the game to stop. She expected an able-bodied person to run out and rescue the player on the ground. Instead, nothing happened. The game continued, with other players grabbing the ball and bouncing it as they moved on down the court. For the first time in her life, Driscoll had truly found something competitive she could do. Playing hard, she was thrown out of her chair twice before the game was over.

Driscoll had been born with spina bifida, a neural tube defect that affects the spinal cord and its protective coverings. When younger, Driscoll had special therapeutic shoes and braces to walk, but when she got older, despite many painful operations, she needed a wheelchair.

Driscoll never looked back after her initiation into competitive sports. She was determined to compete as an athlete of the finest caliber. Driscoll's efforts made people pay attention, with the result of her being recruited by the University of Illinois for its athletic program. Driscoll competed in swimming, track, and basketball. She went on to compete in marathons and set world records for the grueling, 26-mile, 385-yard-long (42 km) endurance race. Between 1990 and 2000, Driscoll won the Boston Marathon eight times.

# Marathon Training Journal

*January 17, 2008*

*My training for the Boston Marathon continues. My inspiration is eight-time winner Jean Driscoll. Driscoll's world-record times for that race have been around one hour and 32 minutes. Contrast that to Bob Hall's time of two hours and 58 minutes. Hall's time might not look as impressive as Driscoll's, but Hall was a record-setter himself. Hall was the first person to ever compete in the Boston Marathon in a wheelchair. At that time no one thought a wheelchair athlete could accomplish such a strenuous feat. Second, when Hall entered in 1975, they hadn't developed the racing wheelchairs like they have today. His chair weighed a whopping 50 pounds (22.5 kg)! Contrast that to my chair's weight of 12 pounds (5.5 kg).*

*February 10, 2008*

*Driscoll can bench press 210 pounds (94.5 kg), nearly twice her body weight. I'm not there yet, but I'm lifting weights three times a week just like she did when she trained. I'm also riding about 100 miles (160 km) a week.*

*I'm a little nervous about the downhill stretches, because it's not unusual for athletes to be bunched together when they go down hills, and speeds of about 50 miles (80 km) per hour are reached. I'll just concentrate on not panicking and remembering that, for safety reasons, a bicycle brake is attached to each racing chair.*

*March 6, 2008*

*Today Coach reminded me about conserving energy by drafting, or following closely behind someone. The racer in front has to overcome air resistance, but the drafting racer expends less energy, because the pocket of air behind the racer in front offers much less resistance. Coach also reminded us about passing rules: I can only pull in front of another racer if I'm at least one full wheel-width ahead of him or her.*

# Show What You Know

*The following are questions based on the passages "When No Whistle Blew" and "Marathon Training Journal." If needed, you may look back at the passages to answer the questions.*

**1. What does one know Driscoll didn't expect of her first soccer game?**

(A) that it would be competitive

(B) that it would be embarrassing

(C) that a big red rubber ball would be used

(D) that players on the ground would be rescued

**2. One reason Hall's time might have differed from Driscoll's is that**

(A) he had a wheelchair that weighed more.

(B) he could bench press twice his body weight.

(C) he trained by riding 100 miles (160 km) a week.

(D) he was the first one to enter the Boston Marathon.

**3. Both stories are about**

(A) wheelchair soccer.

(B) competitive athletes.

(C) training for a marathon.

(D) overcoming air resistance.

**4. When one is forcefully thrown, one is**

(A) drafted.

(B) impressed.

(C) recruited.

(D) catapulted.

**5. From the stories, one can tell that most likely**

(A) Hall saved energy by drafting.

(B) Hall passed other racers in wheelchairs

(C) Driscoll began to train months before each marathon.

(D) Driscoll won her first marathon when she was in high school.

# Show What You Know (cont.)

6. **Fill in the blanks with answers about Jean Driscoll.**

a. What caused Driscoll to be in a wheelchair?

birth defect

b. When did Driscoll expect to hear a whistle?

When some one got hurt

c. Why did Driscoll expect a whistle to blow?

because somethe g of hurt

d. How many times was Driscoll thrown out of her wheelchair?

2 times

e. Where did Driscoll go after being recruited?

Marathons

7. **Write in the date and one fact mentioned in each journal entry about wheelchair racing.**

Date: 1/12/08    2/10/08    3/6/08

Fact: Inspired    training    learning

**Write three or four sentences that tell what each story is about.**

8. **"When No Whistle Blew"**

a person who plays sports in a wheel chair

9. **"Marathon Training Journal"**

Someone who trains in a wheel chair

10. **On a separate piece of paper, write two journal entries, each one telling in part how you are training for a competitive event. The competitive event can be for any type of school activity, athletic, academic, or extracurricular. You may want to include in your journal entries information about the event, past winners, and what you are doing to prepare or kinds of things you are learning.**

# Flying Blood

A doctor needs a patient's blood tested and analyzed as soon as possible. Both the doctor and the patient are on Yeu. Yeu is a small island off the coast of France in the Bay of Biscay. There is not a medical laboratory on Yeu, so after drawing two small vials of blood from the patient, the doctor arranges to have one of the two samples flown to a hospital on the mainland where it can be analyzed. If the blood is not flown by helicopter or plane, how is it transported?

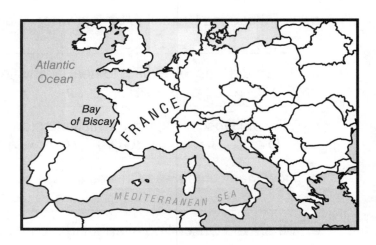

The blood is transported by a carrier pigeon! First, the blood is placed in a red fluorescent pouch. Second, the fluorescent pouch is strapped to the homing pigeon. Once released, the pigeon flies 32 miles (51.2 km) to its home loft in Les Sables d'Olonne on France's mainland. It would take a helicopter one hour to complete this fight, but the average flight time for a pigeon is only 25 minutes.

Once notified that the pigeon has been released, the hospital dispatches an ambulance. Once the pigeon returns to its loft, the waiting ambulance driver removes the sample and takes it to the hospital laboratory. The blood is then analyzed, and the results are telephoned to the waiting doctor.

The vial with the second sample of blood is only used if the pigeon carrying the first sample is delayed. If a pigeon does not reach its loft two hours after being dispatched, it is considered a delay. On the average, about one or two pigeons per day are used to transport blood in the winter months. During the summer months, when Yeu's population triples because of the influx of tourists, as many as six birds may be dispatched per day.

# Scoop of the Century!

Hye Jung told her editor Jerome Patterson, "Don't worry. I'll get the photographs."

Hye Jung's editor looked at his star photojournalist. He said, "Hye Jung, you must remember that you're only as good as your last story, and part of what makes a good story is being first. Sure, you can get the pictures, but so can every other journalist covering the negotiations. To scoop the other newspapers, we need the photographs in time for our first printing. Have you forgotten that for security reasons no cars or buses will be allowed out of the arena until the president and other world leaders are miles away? Unless you can fly like a bird, there is no possible way for you to deliver your pictures in time."

Three hours later, a courier entered the newspaper newsroom with an envelope addressed to "Jerome Patterson, Editor of *The Herald*." The expression on Patterson's face changed from bewilderment to excited wonder when he understood what the envelope contained. "Hold the presses!" he cried. "I've got the cartridge from Hye Jung's camera in my hand!"

That evening's edition, with its front-page picture of the president shaking hands with other world leaders, sold out. "We were the only evening edition newspaper with pictures of the negotiations!" Patterson gleefully told Hye Jung while congratulating her. "It was the scoop of the century. How did you do it?"

"Homing pigeon," Hye Jung said, her eyes twinkling. "After getting some excellent photographs, I raced to my car, where I had stowed a carrier pigeon in a carrying case. I released the bird after enclosing my camera cartridge in a pouch on its belly. Knowing that it would return to its loft, I had directed a messenger to be waiting and to immediately deliver the cartridge to you."

# Show What You Know

*The following are questions based on the passages "Flying Blood" and "Scoop of the Century!" If needed, you may look back at the passages to answer the questions.*

1. **About how much faster does a pigeon get blood to the mainland than a helicopter?**

   (A) about one hour

   (B) about two hours

   (C) about half an hour

   (D) about an hour-and-a-half

2. **For Hye Jung to get her scoop, she had to get her pictures delivered**

   (A) before the presses were stopped.

   (B) before the paper's first printing.

   (C) before the negotiations were over.

   (D) before the president left the arena.

3. **Both stories are about**

   (A) carrier pigeons

   (B) pigeons in France

   (C) homing-pigeon lofts

   (D) transporting pigeons

4. **From the stories, one can tell that carrier pigeons**

   (A) can only carry small vials.

   (B) can be used to take pictures.

   (C) can be used for more than one purpose.

   (D) can fly faster than cars or buses can travel.

5. **If Hye Jung wrote a story about a carrier pigeon transporting the blood of a world leader, for her story to be a scoop it would be necessary that**

   (A) her story was printed first.

   (B) her story had stopped the presses.

   (C) her story was as good as her last story.

   (D) her story had photographs of the world leader.

# Show What You Know *(cont.)*

6. **Fill in the boxes to show what happens when a doctor on Yeu wants blood analyzed.**

| | | | |
|---|---|---|---|
| **1.** B lood taken | **2.** one vial put in fluorescent pouch | **3.** pigon releafed | **4.** hospital notified |
| **8.** doctor telephoned | **7.** blood analized | **6.** pick up pigon | **5.** dispached anbalence |

7. **Fill in the boxes to show the story elements from "Scoop of the Century!"**

| Setting | Characters | Action/problem | Outcome |
|---|---|---|---|
| in a news center | Hye Jung World leaders Jerome ferderson | getting pictures to press | carrer pigeon brings pic. to press |

**Write three or four sentences that tell what each story is about.**

8. **"Flying Blood"**

   This is how blood is sent from a island to france. they send the blood with a pigon. It takes it to france.

9. **"Scoop of the Century!"**

   A writer wants to get pictures to the press. Cars cent leave the area carrier pigon sent.

10. **Describe a way that courier pigeons could be used. Make sure you include information about your story setting, characters, action/problem, and outcome in your writing.** *(Use a separate piece of paper. Your writing should be a few paragraphs long.)*

# Tsunami Survivor

On April 1, 1946, a massive tsunami struck Hilo, a city on Hawaii's Big Island. Although 165 people were killed, 18-year-old Mieko Browne survived. Browne attributes her survival to a pair of dirty shoes.

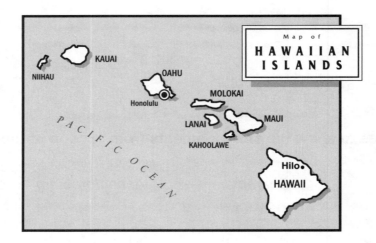

The tsunami was caused by an earthquake near Alaska's Aleutian Islands. A tsunami is a series of huge waves unleashed by an underwater disturbance. Tsunamis are not like regular waves that rise up from the water's surface and crest. Instead, they are like a vast wall of water, reaching down to the ocean bottom, traveling outward from the area of disturbance in all directions.

Browne was about to leave for school, but then she noticed that her shoes were dirty. Five minutes later, after having polished her shoes, she finally left the house. It was then that she heard the warning shout, "Tsunami!" Browne actually believed the warning to be an April Fools' joke until she looked up and saw, in her words, "a huge wall of dirty water."

Fortunately, Browne's mother was able to grab Browne, pull her inside, and slam the door before the 35-foot-high (11 m) wave hit. The force of the water knocked Browne's house completely off the ground, and it began to float. Standing knee-deep in water, Browne opened the door to her closet and saw that the entire back of the house had been swept away. All that was visible were more waves and dead fish.

As Browne saw neighbors desperately clinging to anything they could hold on to, the house was swept three times far out into the Hilo harbor and then back. It was only when the house crashed into a factory wall that Browne and her mother were able to extricate themselves from their floating house and find temporary safety in the factory.

# Hamaguchi's Sacrifice

Yoshi patiently explained to his little sister Mori why a handful of dirt was used to honor Goryo Hamaguchi. "Many lives were saved in our little village of Hiromura because of Hamaguchi's sacrifice," he said. "Hamaguchi was a wealthy landowner. He owned many rice fields high up on a mountain that faced the sea. On December 24, 1854, he recognized the warning signs of a coming tsunami.

"When Hamaguchi saw the ocean pulling back from the land, he knew that the village was in great danger. Immediately, Hamaguchi ordered his workers to set his rice fields on fire. Hamaguchi's workers thought that Hamaguchi was mad. After all, what reasonable man would burn his crops he could sell for a great profit?

"Hamaguchi sacrificed his crops in order to lure fishermen and all the other villagers up the mountain to safety. Hamaguchi knew that everyone would come running to help put out the fire. Thanks to Hamaguchi's sacrifice, countless lives were saved. But Hamaguchi wasn't done with his kindness. When the surviving villagers began to rebuild their homes on the beach, Hamaguchi studied the area and drew up plans for a dike. Hamaguchi paid the villagers to build the protective wall with his own money. The dike took four years to build! Today we honor Hamaguchi and his heroic sacrifice by bringing a handful of dirt to the dike and saying a prayer in his honor."

"Do people in countries other than Japan know about Hamaguchi?" Mori asked.

"Probably not," Yoshi answered. "They probably don't even know that *tsunami* means 'harbor wave.' The phrase comes from the words *tsu* (harbor) and *nami* (wave). The phrase was coined by fishermen who returned home from the deep seas only to find their harbor and villages completely devastated by giant waves."

# Show What You Know

*The following are questions based on the passages "Tsunami Survivor" and "Hamaguchi's Sacrifice." If needed, you may look back at the passages to answer the questions.*

1. **How many times was Browne's house swept into the Hilo harbor?**

   Ⓐ zero
   Ⓑ one
   Ⓒ two
   Ⓓ three

2. **When one is lured, one is**

   Ⓐ tricked or grabbed.
   Ⓑ drawn in or enticed.
   Ⓒ visible or polished.
   Ⓓ swept away or floating.

3. **What do both stories have in common?**

   Ⓐ devastating waves
   Ⓑ sacrificing waves
   Ⓒ waves that hit in the 1900s
   Ⓓ waves that people knew were coming

4. **Most likely, if Browne had looked out into the harbor before the tsunami hit, she would have**

   Ⓐ not polished her shoes.
   Ⓑ tried to lure people to higher ground.
   Ⓒ seen the ocean pulling back from the land.
   Ⓓ known that it wasn't an April Fools' joke.

5. **One can tell from the stories that the tsunami that destroyed Hiromura**

   Ⓐ started near the water's surface.
   Ⓑ may not have started close to Japan.
   Ⓒ destroyed the dike the villagers built.
   Ⓓ was not as devastating as the one that hit Hilo.

# Show What You Know *(cont.)*

6. **Use the clues from "Tsunami Survivor" to mark on the map close to where the tsunami began and where Browne felt it. Put a star (★) where the tsunami began. Put an X where Browne felt the tsunami.**

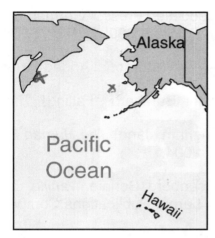

7. **Number the events from "Hamaguchi's Sacrifice" so that they are in the correct sequence of when they occurred.**

| | |
|---|---|
| __2__ orders given to set rice fields on fire | __4__ villagers start to rebuild |
| __7__ handful of dirt brought to dike | __1__ ocean pulls away from land |
| __3__ villagers run to help put out fires | __6__ villagers paid to build dike |
| __5__ plans drawn up for dike | |

**Write three or four sentences that tell what each story is about.**

8. **"Tsunami Survivor"**

A peoson that sarvioed a tsunami.
Thas is because they were wordde

9. **"Hamaguchi's Sacrifice"**

Hamaguchi saw signs of a tsunimai
He saved the vilage.
He paid for a dike.

10. **Think of a holiday or something you do specially on a holiday. Explain the holiday or what you do on the holiday to someone who may not know.** *(Use a separate piece of paper. Your writing should be a few paragraphs long.)*

# Bibliography

Associated Press. "German Shepherd Dials 911 to Save Owner." http://www.hearldnet.com/article/20080915/NEWS02/709159912/-1/NEW. 16 September 2008.

————. "Memorial Added for Late Gold Medalist." *Journal and Courier*. 12 August, 2008: A2.

Bilger, Burkhard. "Falling." *The New Yorker*. 13 August, 2007: 58-67.

Bingham, Jane. *The Human Body: From Head to Toe*. Heinemann Library, Reed Elsevier Inc., 2004.

Busenberg, Bonnie. *Vanilla, Chocolate, & Strawberry: The Story of Your Favorite Flavors*. Lerner Publications Company, 1994.

Capaldi, Gina. *A Boy Named Beckoning: The True Story of Dr. Carlos Montezuma, Native American Hero*. Carolrhoda Books, 2008.

Child, Greg. "Masters of Understatement." *The Mountaineers Anthology Series, Vol. 1: Glorious Failures*. The Mountaineers Books, 2001.

Driscoll, Jean, Janet and Geoff Benge. *Determined to Win: The Overcoming Spirit of Jean Driscoll*. WaterBrook Press, Random House, Inc., 2000.

Foster, Ruth. *A Word a Week Vocabulary Program*. Teacher Created Resources, Inc., 1999.

————. *Nonfiction Reading Comprehension: Social Studies, Grade 4*. Teacher Created Resources, Inc., 2006.

————. *Take Five Minutes: Fascinating Facts about Geography*. Teacher Created Resources, Inc., 2003.

Goodman, Jim. *Thailand*. Marshall Cavendish, 2002.

Gorrell, Gena K. *Catching Fire: The Story of Firefighting*. Tundra Books, 1999.

Herbst, Judith. *Hoaxes*. Lerner Publications Company, 2005.

Hirschmann, Kris. *Killer Whales*. KidHaven Press, The Gale Group, Inc., 2004.

Johnson, Rebecca L. *Nanotechnology*. Lerner Publications Company, 2006.

Keenan, Sheila. *Animals in the House: A History of Pets and People*. Scholastic, Inc., 2007.

Kent, Jacqueline C. *Women in Medicine*. The Oliver Press, Inc., 1998.

Kriek, Jim. "John Woodruff, Connellsville's Olympic Champion." http://www.fay-west.com/connellsville/historic/woodruff.php. 13 August 2008.

# Bibliography (cont.)

Lasky, Kathryn. *Born in the Breezes: The Seafaring Life of Joshua Slocum.* Orchard books, Scholastic Inc., 2001.

Lehrer, Jonah. "The Eureka Hunt." *The New Yorker.* 28 July, 2008: 40–45.

Little, James R. *Wheelchair Road Racing.* RiverFront Books, Grolier Publishing, 1998.

Magliozzi, Tom and Ray, and Doug Berman. *A Haircut in Horsetown and Other Great Car Talk Puzzlers.* The Berkley Publishing Group, Penguin Putnam, Inc., 1998.

Mason, Paul. *Investigating UFOs.* Heinemann Library, Reed Elseiver, Inc., 2004.

Miller, Raymond H. *Stan Lee.* Kidhaven Press, Thomson Gale, 2006.

Noles, Jim. *A Pocketful of History: Four Hundreds Years of America—One State Quarter at a Time.* Da Capo Press, 2008.

Nyerges, Christopher. "Thirty Years in the Jungle!" http://www.primitiveways.com/jungle_30_years.html. 13 October 2008

O'Sullivan Robyn. *Your 206 Bones, 32 Teeth, and Other Body Math.* National Geographic Society, 2006.

Powers, Dennis M. *Sentinel of the Seas: Life and Death at the Most Dangerous Lighthouse Ever Built.* Citadel Press, Kensington Publishing Group, 2007.

Presnall, Judith Janda. *Carrier Pigeons.* Kidhaven Press, The Gale Group, Inc., 2004.

Pringle, Laurence. *Scorpion Man: Exploring the World of Scorpions.* Charles Scribner's Sons, 1994.

Query, Shawn. "Hole In Crab." *Audubon.* September/October, 2008: 14.

"Right Whale." Right Whale Cetacean Fact Sheet American Cetacean Society. http://www.acsonline.org/factpack/RightWhale.htm. 21 October 2008.

San Souci, Robert D. *Kate Shelley: Bound for Legend.* Dial Books for Young Readers, Penguin Books, 1995.

Sommers, Michael. *Tsunami: True Stories of Survival.* The Rosen Publishing Group, Inc., 2007.

"Tomato." *The New Encyclopedia Britannica,* volume 11: 185. Encyclopedia Britannica, Inc., 1990.

Townsend, John. *Mysterious Disappearances.* Raintree, Reed Elsevier, Inc., 2004.

Vathanaprida, Supaporn. *Thai Tales: Folktales of Thailand.* Libraries Unlimited, Inc., 1994.

# Answer Key

**Unit 1**
1. D
2. C
3. D
4. C
5. A
6. *For people:* crabs on course, cannot move and must play around; *For crabs:* moving vehicles, roads closed and signs put up
7. *North:* spring, summer, fall, winter; *South:* fall, winter, spring, summer

**Unit 2**
1. C
2. D
3. B
4. A
5. D
6. 4 = date in August Woodruff ran; 1936 = year Olympics held; 21 = Woodruff's age when made Olympic team; 6'3" = Woodruff's height = 6 feet, 3 inches; 10 = length in feet of Woodruff's stride when extended; 1:52.9 = victory time (1 minute, 52.9 seconds)
7. *Paragraph 1:* yes, dedication will pay off; *Paragraph 2:* yes, grace of a cheetah closing in on its prey; *Paragraph 3:* begin to doubt, he began to panic; Paragraph 4: no, concentrated on what was obtainable

**Unit 3**
1. D
2. C
3. A
4. D
5. B
6. books, magazine photographs, television documentary
7. a. honest, depth of knowledge; b. curator of famous and prestigious museum; c. cellar deep in Italian countryside; d. women

mashing tomatoes into sauce; e. tomatoes weren't yet in Europe; f. first half of the 16th century

**Unit 4**
1. B
2. A
3. C
4. D
5. C
6. *Best:* carpet tacks—when strewn on deck, surprised and hurt thieves; *Worst:* goat—ate charts, clothing
7. 1. made scarecrows dressed in own clothes; 3. placed in portholes, hatches; 4. pulled on strings as shot at canoes

**Unit 5**
1. C
2. A
3. B
4. B
5. C
6. means 1 billionth of something; used in front of structures or devices small enough to be measured on the nanoscale; origin comes from the Greek *nanos*, which means "dwarf"
7. clot on head, injection in right arm

**Unit 6**
1. C
2. D
3. D
4. A
5. A
6. 2. ignited ground around him; 3. wet handkerchief from canteen water; 5. hugged smoldering ground; 6. tried to inhale thin layer of oxygen
7. *center circle:* Zenaida; *outlying circles:* Yow, visiting out of town friend; Jonathon, friend; Mr. Montgomery, firefighter father; Maggie,

aspiring firefighter older sister

**Unit 7**
1. C
2. A
3. A
4. B
5. B
6. A. Laos; B. Cambodia; C. Malaysia; D. Myanmar
7. *Characters:* king, four counselors, farmer; *Setting*: Thailand, king's palace; *Problem*: award only given for lie, counselors say everything true; *Results:* if deemed true, gets money; if false, gets gold and princess

**Unit 8**
1. A
2. C
3. B
4. B
5. C
6. Answers will vary.
7. *Setting:* Jake's living room; *Characters:* Jake, Grandma; *Action:* Grandma upset Jake is reading comics because she feels they're drivel, nothing to be learned from; *Outcome:* Jake proves that something he read in comic book is worthy of a great leader

**Unit 9**
1. B
2. B
3. A
4. D
5. C
6. *before and after:* solid friends; *during:* could not stand to be around each other
7. (answers may vary) walk to the mainland during low time; live with family; row to mainland; dock boat; walk up stairs; easily get supplies

# Answer Key (cont.)

## Unit 10

1. A
2. A
3. D
4. B
5. B
6. 3 = times blood circulates in body every minute; 10 = systems in body; 17 = muscles to smile; 30 = resting child's breaths per minute; 42 = muscles to frown; 60 = breaths during exercise; 70 = adult heart beats per minute; 130 = infant heart beats per minute; 660 = muscles; 100,000 = times eye muscles contract per day
7. 1. bones, Daphne; 2. blood vessels, Chung Sook; 3. cells, Braden; 4. skin cells, Stephanie and Alan

## Unit 11

1. B
2. B
3. D
4. C
5. D
6. 2. hears engine crash; 3. finds bridge out; 5. goes opposite direction, crossing bridge; 6. reaches station
7. led station men to men stranded in water

## Unit 12

1. D
2. C
3. B
4. A
5. A
6. a. caught rattlesnakes in vicinity, sprayed with paint that glowed under UV light; b. wore chaps made of woven brass metal
7. Adrianna, 2; Adrianna, 5; Kaitlyn, 4; Kaitlyn, 3; hawker, 1

## Unit 13

1. C
2. A
3. D
4. C
5. A
6. cumbersome—weight and many yards of fabric; unsanitary—swept floor and collected grime; dangerous—corsets made difficult to breathe and displaced internal organs
7. Katrina, Odessa, Han-Ling, Odessa, Katrina, Odessa, Han-Ling, Odessa

## Unit 14

1. B
2. B
3. A
4. D
5. D
6. Chris Trott: 911 dispatcher who notified police; Buddy: German shepherd who called 911; Joe Stainaker: Buddy's owner who suffered seizure; Mark Clark: Scottsdale Police Sgt. who told how Stainaker's address was flagged
7. a. 1740s Pennsylvania rat epidemic; b. keeping rodents from Midwestern farmer's crops and seeds; c. protecting California miners from being bitten at night

## Unit 15

1. C
2. C
3. B
4. A
5. D
6. current date plus 28 years
7. *Lily:* likes and thinks creative, "how creative and ingenious her friend was at finding nourishment"; *parents:* first worried, then amused, "she had to work at not showing her own amusement"; *siblings:* didn't believe, "they snorted gleefully"; *doctor:* imaginary but not worried about it, "a normal part of childhood"

## Unit 16

1. A
2. D
3. C
4. C
5. B
6. (answers will vary) began 1999; five issued per year; 10-week intervals; one for every state; in order joined Union; number depends on economy
7. 1. Kamala, state with diamond, Arkansas; 2. Roberto, state with peach, Georgia; 3. Sabrina, state with Braille dots, Alabama

## Unit 17

1. A
2. C
3. D
4. A
5. D
6. a. Air Force captain; b. stratosphere, open gondola of helium balloon; c. 102,800 feet (31,300 m); d. August 16, 1960; e. prevent body

# Answer Key (cont.)

**Unit 17** *(cont.)*

fluids from boiling and stay warm; f. highest parachute jump, highest balloon ride, fastest human speed in atmosphere

7. *One:* opened automatically 14 seconds too early, didn't fill with air, wrapped around Kittinger's neck; *Two:* didn't fill with air, coiled around Kittinger's body; *Three:* reserve that opened automatically when Kittinger was unconscious

**Unit 18**
1. D
2. C
3. C
4. D
5. A
6. 1425: Aztecs conquered Totanocs; 1519: Cortes offered chocolate with vanilla by Aztecs; 1602: Morgan discovers vanilla flavor in own right; 1785: Jefferson is minister to France; 1801-09: Jefferson is U.S. president.
7. Paragraph 2, Victoria, enjoyed at first, grown tired after 3 days; Paragraph 5, Aunt Ruthie, grown tired of; Paragraph 7, Uncle Domingo, can't stand it

**Unit 19**
1. A
2. D
3. A
4. B
5. C
6. parallel: //; intersecting: +

**Unit 20**
1. A
2. A
3. D
4. B
5. D
6. Wassaja: means "beckoning" in Native Yavapai;

Hejelweiikan: means "left alone" in Pima; Carlos Montezuma: after adopted father and ruins near native home

7. 1-Ms. McCarthy, 2-Marcus, 3-Venice, 4-Courtney, 5-Loretta, 6-Patrick, 7-Ms. McCarthy, 8-Patrick, 9-Venice, 10-Loretta, 11-Courtney, 12-Marcus

**Unit 21**
1. B
2. A
3. C
4. B
5. D
6. *Example 1:* who—Hillary and Bates, where—Antarctica, what—dialogue when Bates fell into crevasse; *Example 2:* who—Scott and Bonington, where—Karakorum Mountain range of India and Pakistan, what—dialogue when Bonington discovers Scott's legs injured

**Unit 22**
1. D
2. D
3. C
4. A
5. B
6. 1. signals other members of pod; 2. swims underneath floe; 3. pushes floe up so animals slide down
7. top: orca; bottom: (*any of the following*) fish, squid, seabirds, otters, penguins, sea turtles, seals, sea lions, polar bears, walruses, whales

**Unit 23**
1. A
2. A
3. B
4. D
5. C
6. a. spina bifida, a neural-tube defect that affects the

spinal cord and its protective coverings; b. playing soccer two players knocked from chairs; c. thought able-bodied people would run out and rescue people on ground; d. twice; e. University of Illinois

7. (*fact answers may vary*) *January 17, 2008:* Driscoll won 8 times; Hall the first; developed racing chairs much lighter today; *February 10:* bicycle brake attached to chairs, tend to bunch down hills, speeds of 50 mph (80 km); *March 6:* can't pass unless one full wheel width ahead; drafting saves energy

**Unit 24**
1. C
2. B
3. A
4. C
5. A
6. 1. two sample vials taken; 3. attached to homing pigeon; 5. ambulance dispatched; 6. driver takes vial to hospital; 7. blood analyzed
7. *Setting:* newsroom of *The Herald; Characters:* Hye Jung, star photojournalist, and Jerome Patterson, her editor; *Action:* needs pictures of negotiations before print time; *Outcome:* uses pigeon to deliver pictures in time

**Unit 25**
1. D
2. B
3. A
4. C
5. B
6. *star:* near Alaska; *X:* on Hawaii
7. orders given... (2); handful of dirt... (7); villagers run... (3); plans drawn... (5); villagers... rebuild (4); ocean pulls away... (1); villagers paid... (6)